fifth edition

# Earn College Credit for What You Know

Janet Colvin

CAEL
Linking Learning and Work

**Kendall Hunt**
publishing company

Photos on cover and title page: © iStockphoto.com

CAEL

The Council for Adult & Experiential Learning
55 East Monroe Street, Suite 1930
Chicago, Illinois 60603
www.cael.org

ISBN 978-0-7575-9691-9

Manufactured in the United States of America
10  9  8  7  6  5  4  3  2

# CONTENTS

*Acknowledgments*　v
*About the Author*　vii
*Introduction*　ix

**PART I** The Prior Learning Assessment Process　1

*Chapter 1*　Introduction to Prior Learning Assessment and Adult
Learner Profiles　3
*Chapter 2*　Educational Goals and Other Tips for Success　23
*Chapter 3*　Prior Learning Assessment and Coursework Planning　33
*Chapter 4*　CAEL Standards for the Assessment of Credit　47

**PART II** Transcripts and Testing　55

*Chapter 5*　Evaluation of Transcripts and Training　57
*Chapter 6*　Credit by Examination　69

**PART III** Portfolio Development　85

*Chapter 7*　Learning Theory and Application　87
*Chapter 8*　Portfolio Planning　103
*Chapter 9*　Research, Organization, and Writing Strategies　121
*Chapter 10*　Writing about Learning　133
*Chapter 11*　Compiling Supporting Documentation and Submitting
the Portfolio　145

Appendices　165

*Appendix 1*　Finding Institutions That Offer Prior Learning Assessment　167
*Appendix 2*　Prior Learning Inventory　169
*Appendix 3*　U.S. and International Accreditation　176
*Appendix 4*　Military Transcripts and Resources　178
*Appendix 5*　Sample Table of Contents for a Portfolio of Prior Learning　180
*Appendix 6*　Course Research and Prewriting Strategy　182
*Appendix 7*　Sample Cover Sheet and Narrative Excerpt　184
*Appendix 8*　Sample Three-Part Competency Statement　192
*Appendix 9*　Sample Letter of Verification　196
*Appendix 10*　Sample Faculty Evaluation　197

*Glossary of Terms*　199

*References*　209

*Index*　215

# Acknowledgments

- I salute Susan Simosko and Lois Lamdin, who authored previous editions of the book.
- I acknowledge and give thanks for the leadership of Pamela Tate and Morris Keeton, the current and past CEOs of the Council for Adult and Experiential Learning (CAEL).
- I thank PLA practitioners and leaders who have influenced me.
- Thanks to my students in the College of Professional Studies and my colleagues from Regis University, including Margo Rosencrantz, Fran Kehoe, Bea Jennings, Cyndy Redifer, Mike Zizzi, Larry Seid, and Becky Smith-Eggeman.
- My applause to researchers and authors in the field of prior learning assessment, including Urban Whitaker, Tom Flint, Elana Michelson, and Alan Mandell.
- I appreciate the efforts of the staff at CAEL who launched Learning Counts.org, including Cathy Brigham, Mark Campbell, Judy Wertheim, Kelsey Irish, Dorothy Wax, and all the Learning Counts team.
- I tip my hat to students across the country who talked with me about their experience with portfolio assessment, including Andrew Robinson, Jay Brewer, Ty Rhyne, Antelia Salazar-Ball, Maria Gonzales, Tim Lee, George Dow, and Rachel Baxter.
- More appreciation to Susan Kannel, Jo Winger de Róndon, and Scott Bates for extending to me the privilege of serving as the "contact us" person on CAEL's NACTEL and EPCE partnership Web sites (www.nactel. org; www.epce.org).
- I am grateful to Judith Wertheim and Bob Lovely for their careful review and to Holly Holbrook for her editing.
- I am indebted to Diana Bamford-Rees' leadership that brought this book to completion.

In closing, I've had the privilege of a supportive husband, daughter, parents, family members, and group of friends, and a big God.

I believe the growth in prior learning assessment programs in higher education will inspire more students to earn college credit for what they know.

Janet Colvin
Wheat Ridge, Colorado
March, 2012

## Note on the Format

Since I answer a large volume of inquiries from students on prior learning assessment from CAEL partnership Web sites, I decided to use a FAQ-style question and answer format for the book. I believe that most busy adults appreciate reading answers to the most commonly asked questions about prior learning assessment.

This book does not take a cookie-cutter approach to portfolio assessment. I recognize that every program and institution has different standards. The methods represented are not intended to prescribe the best approach or best practices.

The excerpt in the Appendix from "Maria" is fictional but is based on actual students' experiences. The names of people and companies have been changed to respect identities.

# About the Author

Janet Colvin is a respected member of the affiliate faculty in the College for Professional Studies at Regis University, where she teaches online courses and serves as the Lead Faculty for the Academic Resources Department. She holds a B.A. and an M.A. in Speech Communication and is currently pursuing her doctorate in Education in Organizational Performance and Change at Colorado State University.

Janet is an invaluable member of the Council for Adult and Experiential Learning (CAEL) community, facilitating presentations at national conferences and aiding in the continued development of CAEL resources like this fifth edition of *Earn College Credit for What You Know.*

Janet's talents are evident in her efforts to pioneer online courses and teaching practices at Regis University. Lauded for her student-centered approach to teaching and curriculum development, Janet received the Excellence in Teaching Award in 2001–2002 from Regis University as well as a Special Contribution Award in 2006. In 2011, she received a national Excellence in Teaching award from The Commission for Accelerated Programs (CAP). In addition, Janet recently participated in a project for Jesuit Commons to redevelop some of the Regis University online coursework for delivery in refugee camps in Kenya and Malawi.

Janet is innovative, pushing boundaries to assure that students are challenged to reach and exceed their own expectations. She is supportive, providing students with opportunities to explore their own passions and interests. And she is dedicated, willing to share her knowledge not only with her students but with her colleagues as well.

In between her own doctoral classes, her teaching assignments for Regis University, and her personal life, Janet also helps to lead spiritual weekend retreats with Kairos Prison Ministry International at a Colorado prison for women. Janet and her husband John have a college-age daughter and reside in Wheat Ridge, Colorado.

# Introduction

Congratulations! You are about to start an exciting learning journey. You'll be learning about yourself and about how you might already have acquired college-level knowledge and skills. While reading the fifth edition of *Earn College Credit for What You Know* and completing the exercises in it, you will be reflecting on learning that has occurred throughout your life. Yes, you've been learning even though you may not have been enrolled in a school. Your learning may have occurred in the workplace, in informal settings, in your volunteer activities and hobbies, or in the military—and much of it may be college-level learning. This book will teach you how to review and assess that learning, how to find out whether it is at the college level, and how to present it for evaluation by a faculty member.

The Council for Adult and Experiential Learning (CAEL) is proud to produce the fifth edition of *Earn College Credit for What You Know*. Everything we do at CAEL supports one goal: Making it easier for people to get the education and training they need. We do this by finding practical ways to link education to jobs and future careers. We also champion pathways that link learning from work and life experiences to educational goals—so you can earn your degree and credentials faster.

Evaluating learning from experience is typically called prior learning assessment (PLA). Since 1974, CAEL has been a leader in PLA. We train faculty, staff, and administrators in colleges and universities to implement and monitor PLA programs, help students clarify and document their prior learning activities, and investigate the value of PLA. In a recent nationwide study of PLA, CAEL found that adults who had earned credit for their prior learning had better graduation rates than those who had not earned PLA credit. In addition, we found that adults with PLA credit, in general, saved time in earning their degrees.[1]

---

[1] Klein-Collins, R. (2010). *Executive summary for fueling the race to postsecondary success: A 48-institution study of prior learning assessment and adult student outcomes*. Chicago, IL: CAEL.

Because you're reading this book, you're already exploring ways to earn your degree or credential, and there's a good chance that PLA can help you to achieve your educational goals. In addition, reflecting on your prior learning and practicing how to present it for evaluation will not only help you in your education, but also help you meet your career goals. After reading *Earn College Credit for What You Know* and doing the exercises, you will be able to produce a comprehensive profile of your skills and knowledge that greatly supplements and expands upon a chronological résumé. You may also uncover related skills you never thought you had. Clearly describing these skills and how you acquired them can help you identify your strengths for your employer and, ultimately, help you advance in your career.

CAEL produced the first edition of *Earn College Credit for What You Know* in 1985. Since then, we have continued to update and revise it, making sure that it remains current and keeps pace with changes in the assessment arts. The fifth edition, the one you are now reading, follows this tradition. It includes many references to current Internet resources and assumes that many of you will want to use your computers as frequently as possible. Moreover, this edition breaks new ground: it is available both as a book in print and an e-book. Whichever format you have chosen, CAEL is confident that you—like thousands of adults before you—will find the book enormously helpful as you move forward in pursuing your educational and career goals and earning college credit for what you know.

Enjoy your journey!

Judith B. Wertheim
Vice President for Higher Education Services
CAEL

# PART

# I

# The
# Prior Learning
# Assessment
# Process

# Introduction to Prior Learning Assessment and Adult Learner Profiles

Thousands of **adult learners** have successfully used a variety of **assessment** methods to earn **college credit** for what they know. Consider these students' experiences:

- Andrew thought he would feel out of place when he returned to college as an adult. He had quit college when he was younger in order to provide income for his family. Twenty years later, Andrew enrolled in a program that was tailored to working adults, and he found the college atmosphere exhilarating. After learning about the **portfolio** method of earning college credit for his prior **learning**, Andrew earned a total of 32 credit hours in such areas as psychology, video production, and public speaking. The portfolio method provided momentum for Andrew to pursue his educational goals. After finishing his **bachelor's degree**, Andrew completed his master's degree and is currently pursuing a doctorate.

- After receiving **tuition benefits** through his workplace, Tim was ready to earn his bachelor's degree, the piece of paper that kept him from achieving the same success as his colleagues at a software development company. After several years of starting and quitting college, Tim was determined to finish. He received 14 credits for military training, passed a **College Level Examination Program® (CLEP)** exam for a total of six credits, and passed a three-credit in-house college challenge exam in UNIX. Tim earned 13 credits through the portfolio method for his broad experiences in Web development, process mapping, business communication, and project management. He benefited from the **American Council on Education's (ACE)** College Credit Recommendation Service to earn credit for a computer certification. These methods earned Tim a total of 37 college credits—the equivalent of more than a full year of credits toward his bachelor's degree.

- Maria thought her years working out of her home as a licensed day care provider while she was a stay-at-home mom and as an educator in two nonprofit settings wouldn't hold much value toward the **associate degree** she desired. However, after consulting with an **academic advisor** and **petitioning** for credit through the portfolio method, she earned a total of 11 credits for her learning in first aid, early childhood education methods, comparing cultures, communication, and introductory piano. Maria applied six credits toward her **degree** by passing a Spanish CLEP exam; this quickly moved her 17 credits closer to completion of her associate degree.

- Chris is in the military and stationed overseas. She has passed several CLEP and **DSST** exams for 18 total credit hours while in military service. The online college she plans to enroll in will accept these exams for college-level credit. In addition, she will use the ACE-reviewed credit recommendation for military science and then begin her portfolio when accepted into the **university**. Chris anticipates completing the equivalent of one year of college credit when she starts courses next year.

The experiences of these adult students, who represent just a few of the millions worldwide, reinforce the notion that learning outside the college classroom is valuable, lifelong, and, in some cases, useful for earning college credit. In fact, according to the Lumina Foundation (2005), "only one in six students fits the mold of the 'typical' 18-year-old who enrolls at a residential campus, stays four years, and graduates with a baccalaureate degree. Adult students (25 years of age and older) are becoming the new majority". In subsequent research of adults in college, the findings from the University Professional and Continuing Education Association (2010) give evidence to the "changing landscape" of college enrollments: The "new majority" is now portrayed as "89% of undergraduates at both public two-year and private for-profit colleges are non-traditional students. Non-traditional students comprise 57% of undergraduates at four-year public colleges and 50% of undergraduates at private nonprofit colleges." The testimonies in this book not only support this research but also demonstrate how adults who have returned to college have used their rich storehouses of learning experiences to earn college credit toward their degree.

While **prior learning assessment** may be of particular interest to the growing number of adults returning to school, PLA is not age specific. The PLA process and possible credit earned can be just as rewarding and advantageous for the younger student population (Brigham & Klein-Collins, 2010, p. 6). *Earn College Credit for What You Know* is intended to help adult students prepare to earn college credit for their lifelong learning. The assessment methods described in this book represent valid, yet often underused, methods of earning credit. Until more students take advantage of prior learning assessment methods, millions of potential credit hours may remain unclaimed.

# College Costs

Obtaining a college degree is beneficial in an unstable job market. Many of today's jobs didn't exist seven years ago, and it follows that today's knowledge will become outdated; in addition, outsourcing has affected manufacturing, technical, and even medical professionals. According to Morton Bahr (2002), president of the Communications Workers of America, "Training and education will become even more important for workers, especially in tough economic times. Skills and knowledge give people career mobility so that they aren't just left on the scrap heap when a company goes under or announces a layoff" (para. 17).

Consider these numbers from the U.S. Bureau of Labor Statistics (2010):

- Education pays off in both higher weekly earnings and lower unemployment rates.
- The median weekly earnings in 2009 were $626 for a high school **graduate** compared to $761 (associates degree) and $1,025 (bachelor's degree).
- High school graduates averaged a 9.7% unemployment rate compared to 6.8% (associates degree) and 5.2% (bachelor's degree).

Both the U.S. and world economies suffered during the last five years, resulting in job loss. In the short term, economic recovery will be slow. In the long term, many jobs, such as health care, will have shortages. In the long term, a high school **diploma** will not be enough. According to the Georgetown University Center on Education and the Workforce, "the 14.4 million newly created jobs through 2018 will overwhelmingly require secondary education" (Carnevale, Smith & Strohl, 2010, p. 70). Further projections of job and education requirements through 2018 show:

- 63% of the total job openings (46.8 million new and replacement jobs) between 2008–2018 will require at least some college education (p. 119).
- The percentage of the U.S. workforce requiring some level of postsecondary education is up from 28 percent in 1973 to 59 percent in 2007 and is expected to increase to 63 percent by 2018 (pp. 14–15).

According to the **College Board**'s 2010 reports *Trends in College Pricing and Trends in Student Aid,* public four-year colleges cost $7,605 per year in tuition and fees (average for in-state students). A private nonprofit four-year college averages $27,293 per year in **tuition** and **fees**. A public two-year college costs $2,713 on average per year in tuition and fees. However, the total price of a college education may be reduced considerably when students use prior learning assessment. A private college that allows students to earn credit through prior learning assessment may be as affordable as a public college.

## PLA Pays Off! CAEL National Survey on Prior Learning Assessment

The **Council for Adult and Experiential Learning (CAEL)** is a national nonprofit organization that creates and manages effective learning strategies for working adults. CAEL (pronounced "Kale") conducted a study funded by Lumina Foundation. The study examined data for 62,475 adult students at 48 colleges and universities across the U.S. and found that students with PLA credit completed degrees within a much faster timeframe and had higher persistence rates than students without such credit. PLA students also had higher completion rates—actually completing their programs and earning their degrees—as shown below.

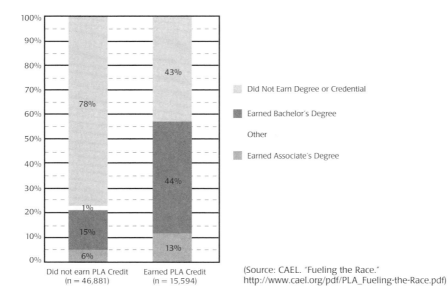

(Source: CAEL. "Fueling the Race." http://www.cael.org/pdf/PLA_Fueling-the-Race.pdf)

# What Else Did the Report Discover?

### PLA saves time.

Students saved on average between 2.5 and 10.1 months for bachelor's degrees and up to 4.5 months for associate degrees.

### PLA Students and graduation rates.

The differences in the graduation rates for PLA and non-PLA students varied based on the policies of the colleges. As an example, at the colleges where PLA credits can be used to gain advanced standing, PLA students were 4 times likelier to graduate than were their non-PLA peers (56% to 13%).

### PLA students stay in college longer.

Fifty-six percent of the PLA students who entered college between 2001 and 2002 but had not earned a degree by 2008 had accumulated 80% of the credits they needed for a degree (compared to non-PLA students who accumulated only 22%).

### PLA students have higher cumulative grade point averages (GPAs) than those who do not use PLA.

Seventy percent of PLA students had GPAs of 3.0 or higher, compared to 64% of non-PLA students; and 98% of PLA students had cumulative GPAs of 2.0 or higher, compared to 88% of non-PLA students.

### CAEL and LearningCounts.org.

In response to the findings of this report, CAEL, cooperating with CLEP®, and ACE, launched LearningCounts.org. LearningCounts.org is a resource to help people identify the knowledge they have acquired through experience, present that knowledge, and earn college credit for it. Included in Learning Counts.org is CAEL 100, a course to help identify and reflect on all areas of learning and build a portfolio that will be assessed by faculty experts. Go to www.learningcounts.org for more details.

# What Is Prior Learning Assessment?

*Prior Learning Assessment* (PLA) or the *Assessment of Prior Learning* (APL) are the terms used by colleges to describe the process of earning college credit from learning "acquired through work experience, employer training programs, independent study, non-credit courses, volunteer or community service, travel, or non-college courses or seminars" (Hart & Hickerson, 2009, p. 2). The assessment methods used work in concert with coursework to help complete a student's educational goals. The process measures the quality and level of a student's **experiential learning**—learning that is based on experience (Kolb, 1984, see Chapter 7 for a discussion of learning theory).

PLA is an active process that helps students determine what they know and what they need to learn through coursework. In the process, students gain confidence in their ability to work at a **college level**. The credits earned also puts them closer to graduation. Additionally, the active process of unpacking the learning reveals insights into areas such as writing, communication, business, and problem-solving skills.

PLA recognizes that adults bring tremendous assets to the classroom because they have more professional and personal experience, have a desire to learn, are more willing to ask questions for a deeper understanding, and typically achieve higher grades than traditional-aged college students.

PLA recognizes that learning is a lifelong activity. The average lifespan in the U.S. is now into the 80s. Since learning occurs throughout the lifespan, no student is too old to finish a college degree.

## What Assessment Methods Are Commonly Used?

Assessment methods vary (see Box 1.1 below), depending on the college and subject matter. The ideal assessment of a candidate's prior learning would require evaluators to look into their students' past; to shadow them as they applied skills, knowledge, and abilities in action; to ask questions to help synthesize their learning; and, finally, to determine if the learning is the equivalent of college-level learning. Since this type of assessment would be

### BOX 1.1   Assessment Methods

- Credit by examination
- Development of a portfolio of prior learning with supporting documentation
- Transfer credit evaluation
- Training and certifications evaluation
- Placement exams
- Simulations
- Interviews
- Work sample evaluation
- Demonstration
- Prepared speeches
- Interviews

impossible and far too time-consuming, colleges have depended on both national and local assessment strategies to determine credit. (*Colleges* is the term used in this book to describe institutions of higher education and refers to both colleges and universities.) Box 1.1 lists several assessment methods. Some are standardized and measure general knowledge; others, such as simulations, are designed to measure a specific competency such as a medical or technical skill.

Assessment methods help reduce students' frustrations by placing them in the correct level. After all, if an advanced performer were placed in a beginning **course**, he or she would likely feel frustrated at the repetition of instruction on the basics. The assessment process provides very useful information for the student because it helps determine what students already know and can do as well as identify gaps in their learning.

## Do I Need to Be Enrolled in a College and Working Toward a Degree or Certificate to Benefit from Prior Learning Assessment?

Generally, yes. To gain the maximum benefit for earning college credit for prior learning, students should first enroll in a two- or four-year degree or **certificate** program. Using assessment methods without having an educational plan is risky, especially if students want to transfer credit. On occasion, businesses, nonprofits, or government agencies use assessment methods when an employee or job candidate needs to prove college-level learning in a subject matter. Or, in rare cases, assessment methods are used for professional development. However, the majority of students who benefit from the methods described in this book are adult students enrolled in a college and working diligently toward their educational goal (see Chapters 2 and 3 on setting educational goals and plans).

## What Is a Portfolio of Prior Learning?

One of the most accepted methods of earning credit involves compiling a portfolio of prior learning. A portfolio is "a formal communication, presented by the student to the college, as part of a petition requesting credit or recognition for learning outside the college classroom. The portfolio must make its case by identifying learning clearly and succinctly, and it must provide sufficient supporting information and documentation so that faculty can use it, alone or in combination with other evidence, as the basis for their evaluation" (Lamdin, 1992, p. 84). Although completing a quality portfolio is challenging, students describe this process as highly rewarding, and, in fact, many students keep and treasure their portfolio work (see Chapters 7–11 on the portfolio method).

## What Subjects Are Assessed through the Portfolio Method?

Since the basis of a student's portfolio is his or her experiential learning, courses that can draw on firsthand experience, reflections, and experimentation work best. College courses or **competencies** weighted more heavily in theory, definitions, and concepts are better suited for testing or coursework. Many colleges' Web sites list the most commonly petitioned courses in their programs. Although work experience is the most frequently used **context** to demonstrate learning, students have received credit for volunteer and civic work, religious and spiritual pursuits, and artistic accomplishments. The list of subject areas may include (but is not limited to):

*Business:* introduction to business, supervision, sales, marketing, finance, project management, human resources, advertising and promotion, managing a small business, customer service, using technology for business, performance appraisals, paralegal courses, retail

*English and communications:* technical writing, business writing, conflict resolution, public speaking, interviewing, public relations, teambuilding, telecommunication, instructional development

*Arts:* photography, music, drawing, painting, art appreciation, jewelry

*Computer science:* computer fundamentals, database, programming, telecommunication, software competencies, Web design, networking

*Social sciences:* applied psychology, intercultural and ethnic studies

*Education:* children's literature, literacy, special education, methods

*Miscellaneous:* records or office management, sports/coaching, electronics

## How Does the Prior Learning Portfolio Differ from Other Types of Portfolios?

The prior learning portfolio consists of written explanations that demonstrate competency targeted to a subject matter area. Also, the prior learning portfolio contains **supporting documentation**—such as letters, certificates, and work samples—to verify that learning. Depending on the level or subject matter being petitioned, students "leaven the mix with ample portions of reflection . . . The learning is not complete until the learner has some understanding of what both the theory and the practical experience mean" (Whitaker, 1989, p. 14). Portfolio contents are compiled in notebooks, or in some cases, saved electronically on a portfolio Web site. When completed, the portfolio is sent to an evaluator or an assessment team that determines the credit award. Commonly, portfolios are used to petition for course credit. However, some colleges may only grant partial credit for specifically defined components of learning, while others award multiple credits for a block of college-level learning demonstrated in the portfolio. The amount of credits earned and for what can differ from college to college depending on their PLA portfolio policies.

## How Do I Know If My Learning Is College Level?

There are several determinants used to measure whether a student's learning is college level. Course outcomes (what is learned as a result of taking a course) are one measure of whether a student has achieved college-level learning. Course descriptions and course syllabi also give clues about the topics covered and level of learning required. Yet another good source to assess your college-level learning could be a recent textbook in the field, which will often contain chapter-by-chapter "course objectives" in addition to topics to be covered and the learning outcomes expected. Students who take exams can review study guides or, in some cases, take sample tests. In addition, instructors and **academic advisors** at the college are skilled in recognizing competency levels and helping students determine college-level learning. Ultimately, a trained evaluator makes the final credit decision.

## How Much Credit Can I Earn?

The amount of credit a student can earn varies. According to the 2010 CAEL report "Fueling the Race to Postsecondary Success," the average number of credits earned through all PLA methods was 17.6. The determination on the number of credits that a student can earn is influenced by both external and internal factors. External factors include the number and level of courses that need to be completed for the degree, the **major** and **minor** selected, and the institution's policies. Internal factors include the ability of the student to demonstrate her or his level of learning.

Some students accomplish a large portion of their **degree plans** through assessment. Students who earn large amounts of credit (21 credits or more) are frequently enrolled in a bachelor's degree program, transfer fewer credits, draw from a large storehouse of learning and documentation, and are highly motivated to complete the challenges of assessment.

*One of the themes repeated throughout this book is that policies vary.* There are national guidelines followed by accredited colleges for awarding credit (see Chapter 4); however, colleges have the freedom to adopt their own policies to meet the needs of their programs. Therefore, it is essential that students always check and re-check with an academic advisor before proceeding with prior learning assessment.

## What Are the Fees for Assessment?

**Assessment fees** vary depending on the assessment methods and the college. Generally, assessment costs less than tuition—in some cases, 70% less than tuition fees. However, there are some schools that charge the same for assessment as for enrolling in a course. Some colleges add a small fee for transcription in the **registrar**'s office (the campus location where the credit is officially recorded). The cost for credits through the portfolio method can be a one-time lump fee or a fee based on the number of credits petitioned. Some colleges offer a tuition-bearing prior learning assessment course that helps guide students through the steps of portfolio development. Because fees are subject to change, students should seek the most updated information available. Always check with your advisor before beginning the process.

## Who Is Considered a Good Candidate for PLA?

Due to the variety of college programs, it is difficult to generalize whether a student is a good candidate for credit. Below are some general characteristics of prior learning assessment candidates:

- Adult students over the age of 24 with a **GED** or high school diploma.
  Adult students are characterized by self-direction, work experience, and independence.

- Degree-seeking students with unfilled credit.
  The more unfilled credits students have in the degree program, the more likely it is that they will have room to apply credits earned through prior learning assessment.

- Students who have worked under the direction of a supervisor or have worked as supervisors or managers.
  A candidate's work experience might be as a front-line employee, customer service representative, supervisor, administrative assistant, small business owner, paraprofessional, manager, or CEO.

- Learning that can be verified.

  When using portfolio-assisted assessment, the learning must be verified by a written document such as a letter or certificate, or an original **artifact** such as a piece of original artwork. Students are held to a higher standard of proof than a **résumé**.

- Learning acquired that is closely matched to the outcomes or competencies required to pass a college course.

  Students are expected to have acquired at least the same level of expertise as a student who received a passing grade in the equivalent college course.

- Learning that is applicable to a number of contexts.

  The candidate's learning should be transferable to another setting. For example, a student's skills as a supervisor and recruiter were proven to be transferable when he accepted a position with another company.

- Students whose lifelong experience is closely related to their educational goal.

  A candidate who worked as a computer programmer, for instance, could more readily apply credits toward a degree in computer science than toward a degree in education.

- Students who communicate with academic advisors.

  Students who are willing to listen and follow the advice of an academic advisor, mentor, prior learning specialist, or instructor will be better prepared to earn credit.

## Where Can I Find Institutions that Offer Prior Learning Assessment

Appendix 1 provides instructions on searching for colleges that offer prior learning assessment. If a candidate is using assessment methods extensively, it is important to find out the prior learning assessment policies upfront.

## What Are the Benefits of Prior Learning Assessment?

The assessment process is profitable for adult students for many reasons:

### It gives validation.

The first benefit of earning credit for learning is that students receive validation for work and life experience. One student who gained credit through

PLA stated, "I was in the workforce for 23 years before going back to college. Through assessment of prior learning, I took a hard look at what I had actually learned. It was one of the most rewarding and validating courses I have ever taken and gave me the confidence I needed to take the next step into my unknown future" (Dow, 2004).

## It saves time.

Earning credit for the learning gained through one's life and work may speed up the process of reaching graduation. Students are able to save time when they can focus on acquiring new knowledge and don't have to repeat what they've already learned. In addition, the flexibility helps students reach their goals and maintain their sanity while balancing school, work, and family. For students who are not ready or able to plunge into full-time coursework, the process may help them earn credit while working at a more reasonable pace. The use of technology has helped students save time because many adult-learning programs offer Web sites or online portfolio-building courses that provide e-mail access to advising services.

## It saves money.

As stated, assessment saves money because the assessment fees are typically less than tuition costs. In fact, a few students reported that they were able to afford to attend an institution with higher tuition costs. Prices for assessment fees vary, but compared with tuition, 30 credits earned through assessment methods could save from $600 to upward of $10,000 (if attending a private college).

## It helps with career and job development.

Students are finding that the portfolio-assisted assessment process is a particularly beneficial process for career development. In the portfolio process, students identify the knowledge, skills, and competencies they've gained. Students have successfully used their portfolios during job interviews or performance evaluations to demonstrate competencies.

## It improves critical-thinking and reflection skills.

Prior learning assessment requires that students look both backward and forward—backward to reflect, analyze, and sort through past learning to identify gaps in learning, and forward to build on the learning (Whitaker, 1989). One study showed that the problem-solving abilities of prior learning assessment students were superior (compared with students lacking work experience) because of their ability to reason and propose solutions based on life experiences (LeGrow, Sheckley, & Kehrhahn, 2002). The ability to think critically and reflect on experiences, which is a skill gained in assessment, is valued highly in both academic situations and the workplace.

## What Are the Limitations of Prior Learning Assessment?

### There are often limited offerings.

This book describes the most common methods of assessment offered at colleges. Some colleges offer one or two methods; others do not assess prior learning at all, but they may accept PLA credits from other colleges.

### The student receives a limited number of credits.

It is not possible to obtain an entire degree from experiential learning. Most colleges have transfer restrictions and something called a residency requirement, which stipulates that a certain number of credit hours must be acquired through actual coursework completed at the college awarding the degree. In other words, most colleges will not award a degree based entirely on a composite of transfer and PLA credits. Obtaining a degree solely for experience, not learning, is often a sales pitch used by **diploma mills**, not accredited programs (see Box 1.2).

### There are financial limitations.

Students should always check with a financial advisor or their company's reimbursement policy to determine if prior learning assessment fees are covered. Specifics on educational reimbursement policies are often accessible on a company's Intranet. Some government-sponsored **financial aid** loans do not cover fees for assessment but may cover the tuition for taking a prior learning assessment course. However, since prior learning methods are lower in cost than tuition, many students elect to pay the fees out of pocket.

### There are transfer limitations.

There may be limitations on the amount of prior learning credit accepted by another college, so students who are considering transferring their credit should first check with that institution.

### BOX 1.2   Diploma Mills

Warning:
Beware of colleges that advertise degrees based solely on life experience. These providers defraud consumers by charging a fee and sending a fake diploma (see Chapter 5).

### It is often limited to undergraduate degrees.

Prior learning assessment is often part of programs that offer **undergraduate** degrees for adult students—either an associate degree or a bachelor's degree. Assessment options for graduate-level coursework (master's or doctorate degree) are less frequent.

Adults learn a tremendous amount from experience. While these learning experiences may be significant life lessons, they may lack the understanding of the theoretical foundation or principles that are the equivalent of college-level learning.

The process of petitioning for prior learning credit does not guarantee that credit is awarded. However, due to screening and advisement, many students are well equipped to earn college credit for what they know.

### When coursework is the better option.

A returning adult student who aspires to a degree in biology may have the ability to test out of an introductory biology course, but for the major, he or she might be required to enroll in the course "Biology for MAJORS." This course would better prepare the student for subsequent coursework at a higher level (e.g., if the student desires to go on to get a medical degree). And if the student did test out, the student would not, under usual circumstances, be able to "double-count" the courses.

## How Is This Book Organized?

This book is divided into four sections:

### Part I: The Prior Learning Assessment Process

Chapters 1–4 provide an introduction to prior learning assessment, adult learner profiles, educational goal setting, prior learning assessment planning, and standards for assessment.

### Part II: Transcripts and Testing

Chapters 5 and 6 provide information on ways to obtain credit for **transcripts** and training (Chapter 5) and credit by examination (Chapter 6).

### Part III: Portfolio Development

Chapters 7–11 provide a review of learning theory and the development of a portfolio of prior learning, which is the method of assessment that requires the most guidance.

**The Appendices** provide instructions on creating a prior learning inventory as well as resources, forms, samples, and definitions.

The glossary of terms (or special dictionary), found at the back of this book, will provide you with definitions of key terms: words ("undergraduate"), phrases ("full-time student"), and acronyms ("CLEP"). Glossary terms will appear in bold to help you recognize them. Whenever you come across a term in your reading that is unfamiliar, please refer to the glossary for a brief definition. Most if not all key terms will be explained in greater detail at some point in the book. You can always use the index to find out where.

## REVIEW

- Prior learning assessment can be a valuable complement to college coursework for students seeking a degree.
- Policies vary from college to college, so it is important to work closely with an academic advisor or prior learning assessment expert.
- Commonly used assessment methods include training and coursework evaluation, testing, and portfolio.
- The prior learning portfolio is a method used to demonstrate and evaluate a student's learning.
- The benefits of prior learning assessment include time, degree completion, cost, career development, and critical thinking.

## NEXT STEPS

1. Using the information provided in Appendix 1, conduct an Internet search for colleges that offer prior learning assessment services. Locate the policies for prior learning assessment used by the college you plan on attending.
2. Develop a learning inventory that lists both your formal (e.g., from courses or training) and informal learning (e.g., work experience, self study, volunteer activities). (see Appendix 2 for instructions). The inventory will be a useful resource for planning prior learning assessment.

**Note to the Reader:** The following profiles provide illustrations of adult learners who have successfully used prior learning assessment methods to earn college credit. In some cases, identifying information of the students, names of workplaces, or backgrounds have been altered to protect confidentiality. The profiles represent actual students' experiences based on interviews.

# Adult Learner Profiles

## 1. Adult learner profile: Andrew

**Profession:** Minister

Completed bachelor's degree in an adult learning program.

Obtained a bachelor's degree in liberal arts, with a minor in psychology.

Completed master of arts in communication studies. Currently pursuing doctorate.

### Credits earned through prior learning assessment (semester hours awarded):

**Portfolio:**

*Psychology:* Crisis intervention (2); Pastoral psychology (2); Human interaction skills (2); theories of personality (2)

*Family and consumer science:* Death and dying (1)

*English:* The Bible as literature (2)

*Communication:* Speech communication (3); video production (3); communication in families (3); small-group communication (3); advanced public speaking (3); communication and conflict (3); introduction to organizational communication (3)

Andrew prepared a portfolio totaling 38 credit hours; in other words, he petitioned for, or asked for, 38 credit hours. However, in reviewing the portfolio, the faculty awarded him a total of 32 credit hours. SIx of the credit hours were not seen as college-level learning.

Credit hours petitioned for portfolio: 38

Credit hours awarded for portfolio: 32

**Total credit hours earned through PLA: 32**

*Pace:* Andrew completed his portfolio in three months by working diligently on one portfolio narrative per week.

*Motivation:* When his stepfather became disabled, Andrew quit college to provide income for the family. Twenty years later, when Andrew returned to college, he felt comfortable attending courses with other working adults.

*Process:* Andrew attended a three-hour portfolio workshop offered by the college. After making a list of his skills and knowledge and comparing it with course syllabi, he had discussions with an advisor who helped him think about whether he could meet the course outcomes with his learning. In some cases, the discussions helped him target the best courses to match his learning.

*Result:* Seeking a degree seemed like a long and drawn-out process, so the portfolio provided him with an efficient means to finish. The **learning narratives** (see p. 98) allowed him to reflect on all he had learned, valued, and discovered in his work as a minister. Andrew said he became keenly aware of his **tacit knowledge**, that is, the depth and breadth of knowledge he had from experience. The process also proved valuable when taking coursework because he could add new knowledge and theory to his understanding.

*Advice:* "Just do it!" said Andrew, who is very persuasive about prior learning assessment. He advises students to stay focused on the task and put their primary attention toward getting the portfolio done. He says, "It is essential that you communicate with immediate family members that you will be preoccupied with your learning goals during this process. For example, my wife felt included because I had her proofread my papers. She was also helpful in confirming facts and timelines."

He adds, "I can't emphasize enough how much the reflective writing practice benefited me in my future coursework, including my graduate studies." Now after completing his master's degree, Andrew is pursuing a doctorate.

## 2. Adult learner profile: Tim

**Profession:** Software developer

Completed a bachelor of science in computer information science in a school for professional studies program.

### Credits earned through prior learning assessment (semester hours awarded):

ACE-reviewed credit recommendation: Military science through basic training and military leadership (14)

ACE-reviewed credit recommendation: Microsoft Office specialist certification (1)

Credit by examination: Challenge exam (offered by the university): UNIX (3), CLEP: freshman college composition (6)

Portfolio: managing Internet information systems/Web development/e-mail (4); process mapping and process improvement (3); business writing (3); project management (3); leadership (0)

Credit hours earned for military experience: 14

Credit hours earned with Microsoft Certificate: 1

Credit hours earned by examination: 9

Credit hours petitioned for portfolio: 16

Credit hours awarded for portfolio: 13

**Total credit hours earned through PLA: 37**

*Pace:* Tim devoted approximately four months to reviewing for exams and preparing the portfolio.

*Motivation:* Tim described his motivation as twofold: the degree would give him leverage in a competitive market, and portfolio assessment would help him speed up the process of obtaining the degree. "After plodding along and taking four to six college classes [over] a period of 10 years, I wanted to get it done."

*Process:* Tim completed an online three-credit-hour prior learning assessment course to learn the portfolio method. Since the portfolio required extensive writing, he received reviews from the instructor and submitted his prior learning narratives to an online writing lab for feedback. As an online student, Tim felt that receiving writing feedback electronically was less intimidating than in person. In addition, Tim prepared thoroughly for the **challenge exam** even though he did UNIX programming every day at work. Tim used his study time efficiently by reviewing commands he used less frequently.

*Result:* The combination of portfolio, credit by examination, transfer credit, and coursework allowed Tim to complete the exact number of credits he needed to graduate. Using prior learning assessment also helped him devote more time to the coursework he needed.

*Advice:* "Stay organized," suggests Tim, who tracked his tasks using a detailed project management spreadsheet he created. His game plan also involved gaining support from his boss in order to juggle his portfolio preparation and workload. Tim advises students to start the process early in their educational plan because "I really killed myself at the end spending many late nights editing and completing my portfolio. I had to be creative in managing my time to complete this high volume of work." At his last performance appraisal, Tim was proud to tell his boss that he had earned his bachelor's degree.

### 3. Adult learner profile: Maria

**Profession:** Early childhood education assistant, Head Start program

Maria completed her associate degree in early childhood education at a local **community college**.

*Credits earned through prior learning assessment*
*(quarter hours awarded):*

*Credit by examination:* CLEP: Spanish (6)

*Portfolio:* Early childhood education methods (2); first aid (1); comparing cultures (2); introduction to communication (3); piano class I (3)

Credit by examination: 6

Credit hours petitioned for portfolio: 14

Credit hours awarded for portfolio: 11

**Total credit hours earned through PLA: 17**

*Pace:* The associate degree required completion of 105 credits during six quarters. Maria completed her portfolio one summer when she was midway through her studies.

*Motivation:* After many years of experience as a mother, educator for a nonprofit organization, day care provider, and teacher of three-, four-, and five-year-old children, Maria wanted to learn more about her field and career and earn credit for her 13 years of working with children. Her short-term goal was to become a lead teacher at the Head Start program where she worked.

*Process:* First, Maria applied for admission at the community college she attended and took her placement assessment tests. Next, she completed her first three quarters of early childhood education courses in the traditional classroom. At that point, her advisor recommended that she enroll in the three-credit-hour "Prior Learning Portfolio Development" course.

*Result:* The 11-week portfolio development course she completed gave her flexibility to work independently on the project. The combination of portfolio and CLEP testing allowed Maria to earn her **elective** and humanities credits and focus on her early childhood education coursework.

*Advice:* The goal-setting exercises (see Chapter 2) and chronological record of her work and family experiences since high school (see Chapter 8) helped Maria distinguish her learning from experience. After running a day care, working at a nonprofit organization, and attending numerous training sessions at the Head Start program where she worked, she found that it was valuable to stop and think about her lifelong learning. Collecting letters for **documentation** from former colleagues and clients took several weeks, but she was pleased when the letters arrived in her mailbox. Distinguishing learning from experience was at first challenging for Maria, but with the assistance of the **faculty** members who reviewed several drafts, she was able to strengthen her request for credit. "I'm so proud of my portfolio," says Maria, who stores her portfolio in a zippered leather case in the hope that one day she will show it to her grandchildren (Maria's profile is a composite of several students' experience).

## 4. Adult learner profile: Chris

**Profession:** U.S. army platoon sergeant first class

Credits to be earned through prior learning assessment (semester hours awarded):

*Credit by examination:* CLEP: college composition and college composition modular (6); DSST: introduction to supervision (3), introduction to business (3), here's to your health (3), introduction to computing (3)

ACE-reviewed credit recommendation for military; Chris plans to apply for credit for her military training and experience through the American Council on Education: military science for basic training (3) and additional military training (9)

**Portfolio:** Chris also plans to enroll in a prior learning assessment course to guide her through the portfolio process (3). Then with the portfolio she creates in the course she plans to petition for credit in photography 1 and II (6)

Total PLA credit hours in the planning stage: 21 (note that this number includes her PLA portfolio course, her portfolio assessment, and her ACE assessment)

Total credit hours earned through examination: 18

**Total possible credit hours to be earned through PLA: 39**

**Pace:** Chris is active-duty military and stationed in Iraq. She can take both CLEP and DSST exams at the military base from a certified proctor. She has completed six exams in four months' time.

**Motivation:** Chris read about earning college credit for military training in an article published in the *Military Times*. While serving in the military, Chris is maximizing her time to prepare for and take exams.

**Process:** Chris is not sure what degree she wants (an associate's or a bachelor's), but she wants to attend college.

**Result:** Chris will enroll in an online accelerated university next year that will accept her PLA credits, including her CLEP and DSST exam credit. After she enrolls, she must complete six credit hours at the university before her PLA credit will be evaluated (this policy is college-specific, other colleges may have different policies). Chris anticipates that the combination of ACE, portfolio, and exams will save her the equivalent of one year of college.

**Advice:** Chris encourages active military, veterans, and civilians to take CLEP and DSST exams. She thinks that preparing for and taking the exams helped her get into a habit of studying college-level content, and as a result, she is more confident about attending college.

## CHAPTER 2

# Educational Goals and Other Tips for Success

*"Returning to school as an adult learner was scary at first. I was excited and nervous simultaneously. What I found was that I was respected for the life experience I brought into the classroom. We were encouraged as students to learn from one another and critically reflect on material. It became one of the most rewarding experiences of my life."*

—KRIS, ADULT LEARNER WHO COMPLETED A PORTFOLIO COURSE

## Why Should I Determine My Educational Goals?

The process of goal setting helps students understand the link between career and educational goals. An educational goal is the driver that determines a student's selection of a college, a major, coursework, and, subsequently, the plan for earning credit for prior learning. Therefore, clarifying the educational goal, and the motivation behind the goal, is a critical first step. Most adult students shoulder sole financial responsibility for their education, so they do not have the luxury of waiting a year or two to experiment with coursework before determining their goals.

In the corporate setting, clarifying goals helps team members build vision and momentum. Likewise, determining an educational goal helps students build momentum toward graduation. Goal setting pushes students to exceed their previous accomplishments. Moreover, goal setting gives students passion, energy, and drive when faced with obstacles. Richard Bolles (2011), in his very popular book *What Color Is Your Parachute?*, emphasizes the importance of goal setting: "If you have a vision of what you want your life to be, ever beckoning you on, you have found gold!" (p. 20).

## What If I Don't Know My Educational Goals?

Starting an education means taking steps from goal-setting to planning. If a student feels stuck in the goal-setting phase, it may be useful to consult a career counselor or join a career development group. The old interest inventories many students took in high school are not of the same caliber as the sophisticated inventories now available. In addition, many of the interest and skills assessments can be taken online at a low cost. The most effective results are found when assessment tools are used in combinations (such as the Strong Interest Inventory® and Myers-Briggs Type Indicator®) and interpreted by a career counselor. Even if this consultation period delays the start of college, the time invested is valuable because it can help reinforce or even dramatically change a student's goal.

Career and educational exploration encourages adults to take actions and assures better-informed decisions. Box 2.1 lists ways you can conduct research on specific careers. This kind of footwork is necessary to reaffirm that you are indeed headed in the right direction for you. Ultimately, it will also help you determine exactly what education and training you need. Actions like networking with experts are invaluable not only to gain insight into what a profession truly entails but also because many careers, like forensic accounting for example, did not even exist 10 years ago.

Without this kind of research, you may find yourself in over your head or just plain miserable. Hastily made decisions are often less than satisfying.

## Box 2.1   Actions That Help Clarify Educational Goals

Action steps are an integral part of the goal-setting process. It is the action, the forward momentum, that brings your goal ever closer to reality. Some actions you might want to take in creating your educational goals are:

1. Conducting informational interviews
2. Researching trends in the marketplace
3. Setting aside one night a week to pursue an interest in a new field
4. Joining a professional organization or attending one of their functions
5. Volunteering in a new field
6. Job-shadowing for a day or several days
7. Asking permission and visiting a class at a college you are considering or taking an online class
8. Joining online discussion groups, forums, and networking groups
9. Researching information on financial aid options (such as corporate or military educational benefits, student loans, or grants)
10. Investigating educational options

Some students jump into their education prematurely or after a particularly painful period or a life transition, such as a divorce, death of a parent, or sudden empty nest, when they have not yet fully examined their options or their true desires. According to one career counselor, many students spend more time shopping for a car than researching their career and educational goals even though they are making an even larger investment in time and money. Take the time to know you are doing what is best for you in the best way possible.

Unfortunately, obtaining a degree does not guarantee a job or a promotion. Job trends show that many adults will work as independent contractors for companies rather than as long-term employees. Students should make the best educational decision possible, realizing that the job market shifts dramatically due to many unforeseen factors. Skills gained in college, such as communication, critical thinking, managing projects, and working with diverse teams, are valuable tools in a fluctuating economy.

## How Do I Select a College?

Many colleges can fulfill the goal of providing a solid education. Therefore, it is a good idea to research every option available in a major or field of interest. Research can be conducted using the Internet and books and by making personal contacts. Most colleges, due to privacy issues, do not release contact information for students, so networking through professional organizations or online groups might be a better way to contact students or alumni. To narrow a college search, write a list of the most important criteria (see Box 2.2). Second, narrow the list to a few key factors and find several schools that match the criteria. Third, conduct thorough research of the selections. Take into consideration that many private colleges are affordable when combined with prior learning assessment.

## What Is Distance Learning?

**Distance learning**—also known as online study, distance education, or distributed learning—relies on educational technologies such as the Internet, CDs, or video for delivery. With the availability of the Internet and the low cost of computers, many students are benefiting from taking courses online. According to the Babson Survey Research Group (2010), "over 5.6 million students were taking at least one online course during the fall term 2009; an increase of nearly one million students over the number reported the previous year," and "nearly 30% of higher education students now take at least one course online" (Allen & Seaman, p. 2).

## BOX 2.2 Criteria for Selecting a College

Develop a list of the criteria you will use for selecting a college. Your list may include:

- Major, minor, or certificate offered
- **Accreditation** (see Appendix 3)
- Coursework and instructors who bring real-life learning into the classroom
- Availability of required courses in major (view course schedules)
- Availability of online, distance, or individualized courses
- Cost
- Prior learning assessment options, services, and potential cost savings
- Time to completion
- Preparation for graduate work
- Convenience
- Learning preferences (classroom-based or online instruction)
- Financial aid, loan, or fee-deferment options
- Convenience of student services such as computer labs, library services, child care, and career counseling
- Accessibility and services for people with disabilities
- Applicability of employer's tuition assistance (if any)
- Course offerings in an accelerated or flexible format
- Ability to transfer credit(s) from any previous college coursework
- Other (fill in factors)

When taking courses online, students typically enter a password-protected site that allows them to view the course materials, assignments, instructor's messages, and classmates' **threaded discussions**. Students may post messages at any time during the day or night, but they must adhere to deadlines for posting their ideas to the discussion and handing in assignments. Many students are surprised that the discussions are lively, social, and educational. The growth of online learning has attracted students from a tremendous variety of backgrounds—including students who are stationed in military bases overseas, seniors who don't want to go to classes at night, students with mobility limitations, and students from other countries.

## How Long Will It Take to Earn a Degree?

The length of time will depend on the goal and the amount of credit a student has previously obtained. On the whole, it is important that students set out to receive the maximum benefits from their education; **adult-friendly**

## BOX 2.3 Adult-Friendly Colleges

Consider colleges that provide services for the adult learner such as:

- Flexible courses: evening and weekend classes; independent studies; accelerated, online, and **hybrid courses**
- Admission requirements that require work experience or training
- Academic advising and other support services offered during evening hours
- Prior learning assessment
- Majors designed to support marketplace needs
- Faculty with experience in the field and trained in adult learning models
- Coursework that emphasizes "real-world" experience and application
- Easy access to services

**colleges** may facilitate this (see Box 2.3). But focusing on a quick fix often results in missing the richest learning opportunities. As Mike Zizzi (2003), a seasoned communications professor, writes, "At the heart of adult learning, especially that offered in accelerated formats, is the stretching out of time. For the adult learner, the course 'begins,' retrospectively, at the time of the student's earliest relevant experiences and the class 'ends' . . . well, at best, it never ends; the term may end and the final work may be turned in, but the learning continues to unfold" (p. 359). Zizzi instructs adult students not to race through their programs of study but to work steadily toward realistic learning goals. To rush students during this important, self-rewarding part of life, Zizzi advises, cheats students of many of the benefits of education.

# What Roadblocks Do Adult Learners Commonly Face?

One of the most common challenges is effective time management, especially when juggling several responsibilities such as finances, work, family, friendships, aging parents, household duties, and recreation. Before starting coursework, it can be insightful to complete at least one time-management exercise (see Box 2.4). After all, anything worth doing, including an education, takes time.

Ineffective time management can lead to another roadblock—procrastination, the habit of neglecting to complete tasks that need to be accomplished. Procrastination can result in falling behind on assignments, increased stress,

## BOX 2.4   Time-Management Activities

**Option 1:** Time-management chart

1. Create a handwritten or computer-generated table that lists your waking hours (e.g., 6–7 a.m., 7–8 a.m., etc.).
2. Fill in the slotted times with the activities that you did during each hour. Ideally, keep track of your tasks for several days.
3. Using the information you collect, determine realistically where you could devote ten or more hours a week to your education. Also, determine your top ten time wasters.

**Option 2:** Take action

1. Brainstorm a list of creative options for using your time effectively, such as riding a bus or train so you can do coursework, using an online grocery-delivery service, or reading or listening to tapes while working out on exercise equipment.
2. Try out one or two of your options to see if they are feasible.

**Option 3:** Duties and responsibilities

1. List the responsibilities and duties you have each week, even small responsibilities.
2. Determine which of your responsibilities only you can do and cross those out. From your remaining list, determine responsibilities that you could live without, give less attention, or delegate to someone else.

and rushed work. Most students suffer from procrastination to some degree, but some are overly accomplished procrastinators who, once they start to lag behind, can't catch up. Researching strategies to deal with procrastination and testing the strategies can be useful before the stakes are high.

In addition to time-management challenges, many adult learners feel they have rusty learning skills. Students who know that their learning skills are rusty might brush up on study skills, writing, reading, math, and computer skills before starting coursework. Even learning simple techniques such as prewriting strategies and **mind mapping** can help avoid keyboard block, a form of writing block characterized by staring at a blank screen. Many community colleges and community adult education programs offer low-cost or free workshops and labs with computer programs to help students get up to speed. The atmosphere in the labs is friendly and nonthreatening. Also, many labs are often fully equipped to help students who have learned English as a second language. Finally, many adult-oriented colleges offer introductory courses to help new students prepare for the challenges ahead.

There are additional steps that students can take to get the maximum benefit from their college experience. One step might be setting up an office in the home or finding a workstation that is quiet, comfortable, ergonomic, and well lit. Another step might involve determining the hardware and software requirements as well as the computer skills needed to be successful at selected colleges, especially if considering online courses. Even scheduling an eye examination can be a valuable step because of the intensive reading and computer work required.

Finishing an education is a large undertaking; accordingly, it is important to discuss plans with family members and coworkers. One report showed that "two key persistence risk factors are work intensity and family responsibility" (ACE, 2003, p. 3). Negotiating ways to lessen workload with employers, if at all feasible, is a good idea. The decision to return to school has an effect on family members like spouses, significant others, children, and stepchildren, so it is best to move ahead only with their enthusiastic support. Many of the roadblocks that adult learners encounter, if anticipated, can be addressed.

## REVIEW

- Setting educational goals is the first step in prior learning assessment.
- Time spent in career planning and researching colleges helps students make well-informed decisions.
- When writing educational **goals statements**, the clearer and more specific, the better.

## NEXT STEPS

1. Write your educational goals using the instructions in Box 2.5.
2. Investigate several options for clarifying your educational goals.
3. Try time-management activities to discover your biggest time savers and time wasters.

# BOX 2.5 Educational Goals Questions

Use the following questions to help you start writing your educational goals. You can write several pages or a short synopsis, but the clearer and more specific, the better.

## Goals, Motivation, and Time Frame
- What are your goals?
- Where and when will you attend college?
- Does the college have a program to meet your educational goals?
- What are the reasons (professional and personal) you are pursuing your goals?
- What is a realistic time frame for completing your education?

## Looking Back
- Was there a turning point when you reached the decision to return to school?
- What are the changes that you've witnessed in the workplace, your personal life, and society that have had an effect on your decision to return to school?
- What are your thoughts and feelings about not having finished your education?

## Looking Forward
- What assets do you bring to the classroom that you did not have even 5 to 10 years ago?
- What combinations of emotions do you have as you think about returning to school? Fear? Excitement?
- Where do you see your career headed in the next 5 to 10 years?
- How might you feel if you do not achieve your educational goals?

## Action Plan
- What is your plan to receive the maximum benefit from your education?
- What changes in your lifestyle are you able to make in order to find time for classwork?
- What are several action steps you can take now that will help you manage your time effectively?
- Who will support you in pursuing your goals? Financially? Emotionally? Academically?
- Are there any skills you need to be better prepared for the challenges ahead, and if so, how will you brush up on those skills?

# Case Study: Help José

José is a 41-year-old single dad with two teen sons. He works at a large retailer as a supervisor for a crew and has an excellent rapport with the employees that he supervises. José qualifies for a tuition reimbursement benefit program at work that will help him with college expenses. The company's plan will reimburse the tuition for college courses taken toward any degree at a regionally accredited college as long as the student passes the course with a grade of "C" or better. José earned his GED 10 years ago. Now he is considering going back to school at a community college near his home. He'd like to be a paramedic. José wonders if any of the skills he has gained while working in retail will help him with his dream to someday be a paramedic. He knows that one of the biggest barriers to going back to school will be finding the time to take classes, study, work, and parent his boys. He is also concerned that his writing skills are rusty, since he learned Spanish as his first language. In addition, José worries that he might be the oldest student in the class and that he's too old to return to school. José needs advice.

Based on the case study, what advice would you give José about going back to school? From what you have read in this chapter on educational goals, write one to three tips.

**Hint!** Do you have any tips on time management? Do you think the skills he has acquired in his present work and personal life will help him in his future career? If so, which ones? What steps might you tell José to take next? As you answer, you will tap into your large reservoir of learning from experience, also known as tacit knowledge, which is discussed in Chapter 7.

# Adult Learner Profile

## Maria's educational goal excerpt

I've worked with young children since before my 14-year-old twin boys were born. Years of experience working with children, and raising my own, have taught me that if I want my boys to be more serious about their education, I need to lead by example. My own parents might not have had the educational opportunities I have, but their dedication to providing for our family by working hard in the onion fields set the standard for my own determination. My goal now is to finish my associate of arts degree and then enroll in a program where I can complete my bachelor's and even a master's degree. I know it's never too late to learn.

# Prior Learning Assessment and Coursework Planning

## CHAPTER 3

*"I completed and was awarded 24 hours of credit through portfolio assessment and testing. I had transferred in a considerable amount of credits; otherwise, I would have planned to complete more credit through prior learning assessment."*

—KRISTI, AN ADULT LEARNER

## Why Do I Need a Plan?

Adults who return to college come to the table with a variety of credits, training, and learning experiences that add complexity to determining their educational plans. The degree is the most critical document students will need to meet their educational goals. Planning helps students identify all of the options available to them and creates a process whereby they can effectively and efficiently complete their educational goals. This plan guides all of a student's decisions regarding coursework and prior learning assessment methods and helps students complete their education at a reasonable rate by keeping track of what they have accomplished and what still needs to be done. Jumping into prior learning assessment or coursework without a plan can result in paying for credit not needed or taking a course for which they may have been able to earn credit through prior learning assessment.

Planning helps students stay focused and ultimately creates a satisfying and well-grounded education. One faculty advisor, Margo Rosenkranz, states, "It is important that PLA be woven into the tapestry of the entire degree plan and career path. It is wise to view PLA as a valid means to an end, but not solely as a way to reduce the cost of a college education or a quick method of acquiring credit. Proper planning helps students build a meaningful educational experience" (personal communication, July 1, 2010).

# Who Will Assist Me in Mapping Out My Educational Plan?

Degree or coursework planning is completed with assistance from advisors, who are also known as academic advisors, degree plan specialists, faculty mentors, or prior learning assessment specialists. Advisors are normally assigned after a student completes the admission process and sends official copies of transcripts to the college (see Chapter 5). Advisors may be available on a drop-in basis or by e-mail, instant messaging, or telephone. Academic advisors are specifically trained to understand their institution's sequence of courses, transfer policies, course loads, and prior learning options. See Box 3.1 for a guide to meeting with your advisor.

## BOX 3.1   Meeting with Academic Advisors

Students should not rely solely on the advice of other students or information on Web sites to make educational planning decisions. When meeting with advisors, it is important to:

1. Compile degree-planning information. Review the college Web site regarding majors, courses offered, and requirements. Print out or bring copies of any checklists of requirements and student records. Bring a copy of your learning inventory (see Appendix 2), which will help you refer back to previous education, training, and knowledge that may be relevant to your degree planning. This inventory will also help the academic advisor understand your prior learning.

2. Communicate effectively:
   - In person, be prepared to ask questions, take notes, and write answers.
   - By e-mail, write a detailed and numbered list of questions. Include your full name, program, and student identification number.
   - By phone, identify your full name, student identification number, phone numbers, and available times to talk.

3. Verify transfer credits and course options. Course substitutions or waivers require an advisor's written approval.

# What Questions Should I Ask about Prior Learning Assessment?

Box 3.2 includes questions that can be discussed with an advisor, or the questions may be answered by attending a PLA course or workshop.

## BOX 3.2   PLA Questions

*PLA Methods:*
- What prior learning assessment options are available?
- Portfolio assessment?
- Credit by examination (CLEP, DSST, challenge exams, etc.) (see Chapter 6 for information about these exams)?
- Are course challenge exams available?
- ACE recommendation on training, certifications, and military education (see Chapter 5 for more information on ACE)?
- Other methods of assessment?

*Procedures:*
- Are the procedures and policies for PLA in the student handbook?
- When can I start earning PLA credits? After I am enrolled? After I have completed coursework?
- When can I enroll in a prior learning assessment class, workshop, or program if offered?
- Is PLA instruction available online?
- Is it advisable to take a writing course first?
- Is there a deadline for completing PLA credits (before graduation)?

*Fees:*
- What are the fees? For the course? For assessment? For transcripting the credits I may earn?
- Where do I pay the fees?

*Who:*
- Whom should I contact to discuss PLA options?
- Who will evaluate the portfolio?

(continued)

*Where:*
- Where can I find samples of student portfolios available to review?
- Where can I find handouts or resources?
- Does the college serve as a CLEP or DSST testing center? If not, where is the closest authorized testing center located?

*Policies and restrictions:*
- Is there a limit on the number of total credits a student can earn through PLA?
- What factors influence the limit, such as a residency requirement?
- To which section of the degree program can the PLA credit be applied, General studies, Minor, Electives?
- Is there a limit on the number of PLA credits that can be earned in each category, or in the upper level or lower level?
- Which courses are not eligible for PLA credit: Seminars, Capstone projects, Internships?
- Does the college follow the CAEL recommended standards for assessment (outlined in Chapter 4)?
- Is there a penalty for failing an assessment?
- What areas or subject matter are most commonly petitioned?
- How many credits, on average, do students earn through PLA?
- What will the PLA credits look like on my transcript?

## What Factors Should I Consider When Mapping Out a Plan?

When mapping an educational plan, determine all the credits needed. Once you know all of the requirements, you can explore what assessment options are available, and you will know where you really need coursework to enhance and complete your program. Use the information in Box 3.3 to help you make informed decisions about your course of study.

### BOX 3.3   Factors to Consider in Educational Planning

*Quality of education*
Consider ways to maximize the learning opportunity by taking a wide range of courses or examinations across the **disciplines** while developing mastery in your major or field.

(continued)

*Course offerings*
Consider how courses are offered. Are they offered at a time, at a place, or using a method that allows students to participate?

*Sequencing*
Consider the sequence of the course. For instance, there may be fundamental or **prerequisite** courses that need to be taken before enrolling in another course. If needed, plan on taking review courses in such areas as writing or math.

*Cost*
Consider the possible cost savings of using testing or portfolio-assisted assessment.

*Time*
Schedule time wisely to avoid overload. Since building a quality portfolio is worthwhile and takes time, schedule the activity when coursework is light.

*Prior learning assessment options*
Consider that, during the process of compiling a portfolio, many students are surprised to uncover how much learning they can use to petition for credit. Therefore, the plan should be flexible enough to allow you to discover ways to earn credit through prior learning assessment.

*Preferred learning style*
Consider learning preferences. Determine the best fit. If you prefer face-to-face or hands-on instruction, consider ground-based courses. At the same time, don't place limitations on using distance-education options. You may be surprised at the quality of instruction and discussion available in online forums.

*Accreditation*
Consider the type of accreditation the school holds. Accreditation may be a factor when transferring credit (e.g., credits from a technical college may not transfer to a regionally accredited liberal arts college).

*Graduate studies*
Consider plans for graduate studies and the need for prerequisite coursework.

# What Are the Components of a Typical Undergraduate Degree Program?

The two basic undergraduate degrees are the associate's degree and the bachelor's degree. Associate degrees are often earned in two years from a community or vocational college and generally require 60 credit hours. Four-year colleges and universities may also offer associate degree programs but their undergraduate programming is mostly focused on the bachelor's degree. Both degrees have fundamental elements required for all students.

- **General or core requirements:** Also known as general education, gen-ed, general studies, university studies, core requirements, core curriculum, or group studies. These requirements may include but are not limited to: English, math, natural sciences, humanities, and social sciences. Other requirements may include religious studies or philosophy, computer technology, or international/global studies. General education requirements are necessary for both associate and bachelor's degrees.
- **Major:** Student's primary area of academic concentration. For an associate degree, students usually take lower-division or lower-level courses (generally 100–200 level). For the bachelor's degree, students take both lower- and upper-division, or upper-level, coursework (300–400 level).
- **Minor:** Normally a minor is completed with four or more courses in an area of study. In most bachelor's degree programs, minors are optional; nor are they a required component of associate degree programs.
- **Electives:** Also known as general electives, open electives, or free electives. Used to place any course that is not required by the major or core studies. Required components of both associate and bachelor's degrees.

# How Can I Use Prior Learning Assessment Methods to Meet Degree Requirements?

Box 3.4 illustrates how three students used a combination of methods to fulfill bachelor's and associate degree requirements).

# Adult Learner Profiles

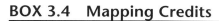

## BOX 3.4 Mapping Credits

### Andrew

Goal: Bachelor of arts degree in liberal arts, minor in psychology

| CREDITS | CATEGORY | NOTES |
|---------|----------|-------|
| 0 | Transfer | Completed courses at a Bible college that did not transfer because the college was not regionally accredited. Learning from this experience identified by advisor as potential for portfolio evaluation. |
| 32 | Portfolio | Combined learning from his pastoral and communication experience and knowledge of communication principles to petition for credit. |
| 88 | Coursework | B.A. in liberal arts, minor in psychology |
| 120 | Total credits needed based on semester hours | |

### Tim

Goal: Bachelor of science degree in computer science

| CREDITS | CATEGORY | NOTES |
|---------|----------|-------|
| 31 | Transfer | Transferred credit from three different colleges. Credit that earned a "C minus" or higher grade was transferred. Credit earned at a technical college transferred as elective credit (not credit in the major). |
| 14 | Military service | Training/service in the U.S. Army |
| 3 | Challenge exam | UNIX |
| 6 | CLEP exam | "Freshman College Composition" |
| 13 | Portfolio | Combined learning from his business and computer experience to petition for credit. (A maximum of 45 credits could be earned through portfolio at this college.) |
| 1 | College evaluation of certification | ACE recommended Microsoft Office Specialist certification |
| 60 | Coursework | B.S. in computer information science |
| 128 | Total credits needed based on semester hours | |

(continued)

**Maria**

Goal: Associate of arts degree in early childhood education

| CREDITS | CATEGORY | NOTES |
|---|---|---|
| 11 | Portfolio | Combined her learning in first aid, early childhood education methods, comparing cultures, communication, and introductory piano to petition for credit. (A maximum of 16 credits could be earned through portfolio at this college.) |
| 6 | CLEP exam | "College-Level Spanish Language" |
| 88 | Coursework | A.A. in early childhood education |
| 105 | Total credits needed based on quarter hours | |

# How Can I Use Prior Learning Assessment to Fulfill Elective Credits?

The elective category is the most flexible category for exploring prior learning assessment credit possibilities. While some degree plans or majors have more course requirements, leaving little room for electives, other plans allow 35 or more credits in the elective category. Since the elective category allows more freedom in the selection of courses, it may be an ideal area to fill with prior learning options.

Creating a plan to fulfill elective requirements is exactly like what you've done to map out possible PLA credits for core and general ed requirements. First, work with an advisor to create a list of the number of electives needed for your degree program. Now list options for earning elective credits through PLA, such as military experience, professional training, transfer credits (covered in Chapter 5), portfolio assessment (covered in Chapters 7–11), and credit by examination (covered in Chapter 6). As before, now you know exactly where you really need coursework. Decide which electives you will take to complete the requirements, always double-checking that you haven't duplicated any credits. See Box 3.5 for an example of one student's elective chart.

## BOX 3.5 Mapping Electives

| CATEGORIES | CREDITS |
|---|---|
| Total elective credits needed for program | 32 |
| PLA elective credits already assessed | |
| Military | 12 |
| DSST exam | 3 |
| Transfer | 6 |
| Total | 21 |
| Possible PLA elective credits to be assessed | |
| Portfolio elective credits | 9 |
| Total possible PLA credits to be used for electives | 30 |
| Credits needed through coursework | 2 |

# How Can I Use Prior Learning Assessment to Fulfill General or Core Requirements?

It may be more difficult to use PLA options to meet core requirements than electives. Core requirement categories, such as English, math, social science, and humanities, have greater restrictions. One way to map out the options for fulfilling general or core requirements is to create a table (See Box 3.6 for ideas).

## BOX 3.6  General or Core Requirements Preliminary Worksheet

Instructions:

1. Create a table or a spreadsheet. List the core course requirements and number of credits needed to fulfill the program. Indicate the courses fulfilled by transfer.

2. Take careful notes from meetings with advisors on options eligible to meet each requirement.

3. Note acceptable exams or portfolio options related to your prior learning.

4. Check with an advisor to confirm that courses are not duplicated—that is, are not used in more than one slot.

5. Verify all prior learning assessment options with an advisor or portfolio specialist.

6. Use the spreadsheet as a process of discovery. The decisions may need adjustment as you uncover your learning during the portfolio assessment process.

7. Construct a timeline for completing prior learning assessment credit.

Box 3.7 shows an example of one student's core requirements worksheet. This student had experience in crisis counseling, interviewing, and organizational development at several nonprofit organizations, so she noted the exams and portfolio options related to her prior learning. There were many more options available than listed in this chart, but working on a preliminary plan was valuable to the learner to help map out the options she hadn't previously considered.

BOX 3.7  Core Requirements Sample Worksheet

| CATEGORY (FILL IN THE REQUIREMENTS) | # OF CREDITS NEEDED | ACCEPTABLE COURSES OR COURSE DISCIPLINES | ACCEPTABLE EXAMS RELATED TO MY PRIOR LEARNING | POSSIBLE PORT-FOLIO PETITIONS RELATED TO MY PRIOR LEARNING | PRELIMINARY DECISIONS VERIFIED BY MY ADVISOR (SEE ✓) |
|---|---|---|---|---|---|
| English | 6 | Transferred English credits from a community college.✓ | | | |
| Mathematics | 3 | Math—college algebra and above. Take math assessment first. | None | None | Take statistics course✓ |
| Social science | 6 | Psychology, economics, history, sociology | "Human Growth & Development " (CLEP), "Fund of Counseling" (DTTS) | Organizational psychology, crisis theory and practice, interviewing | Take portfolio course and discuss options with instructor.✓ |
| International studies | 6 | Language, global studies | French (CLEP) | | Review French and try CLEP exam.✓ |
| Natural science | 3 | Transferred astronomy course from a community college.✓ | | | |
| Philosophy and religion | 6 | Philosophy, religion | None | None | Take courses.✓ |
| Humanities | 6 | Communication, English, humanities | "Analyzing and Interpreting Literature" (CLEP) | Interviewing theory and practice | Interested in expanding my love of literature and will take courses.✓ |

Continue chart for additional requirements.
✓ Checked with advisor.

Ultimately, assessment options depend on an individual's learning experiences and how the learning relates to college-level learning (see Chapter 1's discussion of college-level learning).

## How Can I Use Prior Learning Assessment Methods to Fulfill Major or Minor Requirements?

Students must understand their college's policies. In some cases, students can use prior learning assessment credits to fulfill major or minor requirements; however, there are likely to be more restrictions in this category (see Box 3.8). For instance, prior learning assessment credits may be restricted to fulfilling half of the total credits needed for a minor. Students with extensive experiential learning may have a strong practical understanding of the topic, but they may be limited in their theoretical understanding. Theoretical understanding helps students place their applied learning in a larger

### BOX 3.8  Considerations When Fulfilling Coursework in the Major or Minor

*Sequencing*
Foundation courses help students build a solid understanding for future courses. Sequencing is especially important in fields like nursing or computer science in which the sequence of learning is essential and, if missed, may hinder a student's success. For example, a student interested in a nursing program will be required to take Anatomy and Physiology. In this case, it may be more beneficial to actually enroll in the Introductory Biology course, which will have the most current information to best prepare for A & P, rather than attempt to test out.

*Levels of theory and expertise required*
Students may consult a professor in their chosen discipline or look at course syllabi to help determine whether their prior learning is at the level and depth that is equivalent to college-level courses in the major or minor.

*Plans for graduate school*
Some graduate schools may require that a specific number of credits be completed through coursework, so it is worth checking their policies if graduate school is being considered.

context and builds a strong foundation of understanding for future coursework. Some colleges offer short theory-building courses to students that, when combined with their prior learning, can fulfill course requirements. Ultimately, prior learning assessment is intended to help students measure what they know without compromising their learning in a chosen field. Therefore, students should seek the advice of advisors or faculty members when petitioning for credit in their major.

## REVIEW

- Creating a plan with the support of an advisor helps students to avoid earning more credit than needed to meet their goals.
- There are no ironclad rules for determining where prior learning assessment applies. Students should research all their options and make decisions based on applicable prior learning assessment available, quality of education, time, cost, preferred learning style, and sequencing.

## NEXT STEPS

1. Determine the policies and guidelines for using prior learning assessment methods at your institution.
2. Research and create a spreadsheet of degree requirements and options.
3. Start a list of questions or create a preliminary chart of PLA options to verify with an academic advisor or prior learning specialist.

# CAEL Standards for the Assessment of Credit

This chapter provides information on the standards, principles, and procedures established by the Council for Adult and Experiential Learning in the governance of prior learning assessment. These standards are written primarily with **assessors,** program developers, and administrators in mind, and they speak to credentialing agencies and policy-makers as well. By reviewing and becoming familiar with the standards, you will be better informed and gain insight into the practices of good assessors and the policies that colleges and credentialing agencies have established to maintain high standards in awarding credit for prior learning.

Prior learning assessment is not a "get credit quick" scam but a set of well-established practices recognized by the most rigorous accrediting associations. Becoming familiar with the CAEL standards will help you select quality assessment programs and services as well as help you set your own expectations for what is—or should be—involved in the evaluation of your learning.

## What Are CAEL's 10 Standards for Assessing Learning?

As published in the second edition of *Assessing Learning: Standards, Principles, and Procedures* by Fiddler, Marienau, and Whitaker (2006), CAEL's 10 standards for PLA are

1. Credit or its equivalent should be awarded only for *learning*, and not for *experience*.
2. Assessment should be based on standards and criteria for the level of acceptable learning that are both agreed upon and made public.
3. Assessment should be treated as an integral part of learning, not separate from it, and should be based on an understanding of learning processes.

4. The determination of credit awards and competence levels must be made by appropriate subject matter and academic or credentialing experts.
5. Credit or other credentialing should be appropriate to the context in which it is awarded and accepted.

## Administrative Standards

6. If awards are for credit, transcript entries should clearly describe what learning is being recognized and should be monitored to avoid giving credit twice for the same learning.
7. Policies, procedures, and criteria applied to assessment, including provision for appeal, should be fully disclosed and prominently available to all parties involved in the assessment process.
8. Fees charged for assessment should be based on the services performed in the process and not determined by the amount of credit awarded.
9. All personnel involved in the assessment of learning should pursue and receive adequate training and continuing professional development for the functions they perform.
10. Assessment programs should be regularly monitored, reviewed, evaluated, and revised as needed to reflect changes in the needs being served, the purposes being met, and the state of the assessment arts.

# How Do These Standards Apply to Me?

## 1. Credit or its equivalent should be awarded only for *learning,* and not for *experience.*

Experience can be "an excellent potential source of learning" (Whitaker, 1989, p. 11). Indeed, experiential learning often produces superior learning outcomes compared to direct instruction (Fiddler et al., 2006, p. 1). But experience alone is not considered an adequate yardstick for assessment: in addition, you must make meaning out of your experience. Learning from experience is an intentional process, and intentional learning cycles through phases of doing, reflecting, connecting, and applying your experience. An intentional learner "looks for learning" from experience and becomes able to apply that learning to a number of future scenarios, which may or may not be similar in context. Most of us are intuitively aware that experience is an essential component or starting place for learning, but the process of developing a portfolio asks you to make the intuitive concrete by giving thorough and thoughtful explanations of your experiential knowledge. Experience yields learning when the learner reflects on the experience. Since the distinction between learning and experience is critical to assessment, Chapter 7 provides further explanation of this process.

In addition, the assessment of learning is not a simple calculation based on input—the hours or years spent in experience. "Unfortunately, there is no guarantee that 'X' amount of experience will yield 'Y' amount of learning" (Fiddler et al., 2006, p. 14). Instead, assessment is based on the learning outcome, or the results of the learning.

## 2. Assessment should be based on standards and criteria for the level of acceptable learning that are both agreed upon and made public.

Make sure you know and understand your school's standards and criteria for the level of learning (e.g., lower or upper division, undergraduate, graduate, or professional credential) you are seeking. These standards and criteria should be publicly available and expressed clearly enough to serve as a guide for deciding what you might gather and organize as evidence of your learning. You should understand that colleges and accrediting institutions have multiple ways of defining what their acceptable level of learning actually is. Many prior learning assessment programs require that learning from experience be comparable to college-level course outcomes. Here, CAEL's second PLA standard would additionally require each course to make explicit and public the outcomes that have been determined by academic experts. Some schools also recognize that an exact match of learning outcomes in a course, when compared to learning that a student obtained outside a course, may be impossible; therefore, they have developed, once again with the guidance of academic experts, a variety of reference points that ensure an accurate interpretation and assessment of learning from experience for all levels of learning.

For example, when assessing whether prior learning is indeed college level, the measurement will probably rest on criteria and judgments of the depth, breadth, and complexity—or other characteristics—of the learning. A college is also likely to require that to obtain credit, a student must not only demonstrate college-level learning, but also do so at a comparable or equivalent level of learning to a course at a passing level (e.g., a "C" level or higher).

Because there are no universal criteria for the measurement of learning, there are other criteria you may encounter (see Fiddler et al., 2006, p. 16 for examples). Whitaker (1989) discusses one commonly used criterion for assessment, which is that the learning needs to exhibit a balance, appropriate to the subject, between theory and practical application. He states, "The learning is not complete until the learner has some understanding of what both the theory and the practical experience mean. It isn't enough to have both in isolation; the learner needs to know why they are necessary, and how each extends the value of the other" (p. 14).

### 3. Assessment should be treated as an integral part of learning, not separate from it, and should be based on an understanding of learning processes.

The assessment process itself is a learning process. Quality assessment not only offers students a way to earn credit, it also informs and guides a student's learning. As stated in standard number 2, assessment is based on criteria that are established by academic experts and that are also made known to the assessor and the student; therefore, as students use PLA methods and strive to find how their prior learning meets those criteria, they are learning about their learning. In other words, they are altogether steeped in a learning process. In addition, any feedback received on an assessment, when honestly considered by students, can be an insightful tool for future assessments and learning.

Beyond being a learning process in and of itself, assessment is also based on prevailing learning theories. There are many ways to describe and understand learning (Chapter 7 highlights a few), and these models, theories, and descriptions all have underlying assumptions about what constitutes learning, how learning is acquired, how to define levels of learning, and how to measure outcomes of learning. In turn, PLA is based on the assumptions held by the college or credentialing agency about the nature of learning. Quality assessment programs are characterized by a careful alignment of their understanding of learning with the assessment processes adopted. In addition, how and when feedback is given rest on the theory or model of learning that informs a program's philosophy and practice.

### 4. The determination of credit awards and competence levels must be made by appropriate subject matter and academic or credentialing experts.

Not only are experts necessary to create high quality criteria for PLA, they are also necessary to maintain those high standards during the actual assessment process. Trained academic or credentialing experts—normally faculty and other trained professionals at a college—determine the level and number of credits awarded. These experts know the content area and are also specifically trained in assessment practices. Likewise, examinations are continually evaluated by academic committees or locally trained content experts to set the standards for passing scores.

The portfolio process can be a challenging, albeit rewarding, endeavor, so some colleges offer a course to guide students through the process of creating a portfolio of prior learning. The course may be instructor-led or self-paced. Note, however, that there is a distinction between personnel who coach students and provide feedback in a course or in an advising capacity and the subject matter expert who actually assesses the portfolio and then makes the credit determination. The portfolio building *process* may include guidance from trained experts, but the portfolio end *product* is evaluated by a subject area expert. Some colleges use a blind assessment procedure to evaluate portfolios, meaning that students don't know who will be evaluating their credit until the credit award is completed. In any case, quality programs use trained subject matter experts to determine credit awards so students can't "fake it" by filling up a petition with jargon hoping to cover for inadequate learning.

## 5. Credit or other credentialing should be appropriate to the context in which it is awarded and accepted.

The context for awarding PLA credit is often defined by things like a **curriculum**, personal goals, professional standards, and regulations. Care must be taken to fit experiential learning to the appropriate context (Fiddler et al., 2006). For instance, within the context of awarding college-level learning, most colleges require that students specify how the credit for prior learning contributes to their overall academic objective. Within the context of academic planning, assessment is useful because students look both backward to identify their past learning and forward to integrate that learning into their goal (Whitaker, 1989). Students should expect guidance in how the program interprets this standard so that they can go about the process of developing and providing evidence of their learning in a way that meets the program's expectations regarding "context."

These first five standards have a direct correlation to how you should prepare your evidence of learning from experience as well as how that evidence should be evaluated. The last five standards, on the other hand, focus more on administrative policies and quality assurance of programs. While standards 5 through 10 may not have a direct impact on how you petition for credit or develop a portfolio and how those things are assessed, they are still vitally important. When you understand these final standards, you will know exactly what to expect from quality PLA programs.

## 6. If awards are for credit, transcript entries should clearly describe what learning is being recognized and should be monitored to avoid giving credit twice for the same learning.

Monitoring of credits earned is essential to avoid duplication or "double-dipping" by earning the same credit twice. For example, a student who has received credit for a college-level English course would duplicate credit by taking the corresponding English CLEP examination. Similarly, a course completed in Supervisory Theory and Practice might duplicate an exam in Introduction to Supervision. Traditional titles for courses are often not accurate descriptions of the learning outcomes (Fiddler et al., 2006), so if two or more titles of courses you have taken suggest redundancies, your advisor may request course descriptions or course syllabi to verify that the content of the courses was different.

## 7. Policies, procedures, and criteria applied to assessment, including provision for appeal, should be fully disclosed and prominently available to all parties involved in the assessment process.

As a student, you should expect policies regarding prior learning assessment and credit by examination to be published in the school's catalog and/or on their Web site. You may find, however, that they may only be obtained through a PLA office. In this case, you can contact the registrar's office or prior learning assessment office for the most current policies.

## 8. Fees charged for assessment should be based on the services performed in the process and not determined by the amount of credit awarded.

Fees for assessment are required up front. Additional fees may be required to transcript the credit or place the credit officially with the college's registrar. If submitting a portfolio of prior learning, fees should be based on the complexity of the portfolio submission and the effort required to make the evaluation. These elements are often reflected in the number of credits being petitioned, and so a fee may be based on that figure. Fees for assessment should not be based on the number of credits awarded. One of the important implications of this standard is that paying the assessment fee is not a guarantee of credit.

As stated in previous chapters, fees for credit hours are subject to the policies of the specific college or university. Always check with your advisor before beginning the assessment process. There is no standard pricing for the assessment of learning.

## 9. All personnel involved in the assessment of learning should pursue and receive adequate training and continuing professional development for the functions they perform.

This standard once again assures the student of quality control. Since assessment is a complex process, colleges and credentialing agencies should be continually training and updating personnel involved in the assessment of prior learning.

## 10. Assessment programs should be regularly monitored, reviewed, evaluated, and revised as needed to reflect changes in the needs being served, the purposes being met, and the state of the assessment arts.

The final CAEL standard requires that quality control measures are set in place for programs offering prior learning assessment. Quality programs are continually being monitored and revised, as needed. Because of this requirement, assessment standards and policies are subject to change, so when applying for credit, it is important for students to double-check and follow the latest policies.

## REVIEW

- The guidelines set by CAEL provide standards for quality control of assessment practices. Colleges and credentialing agencies set individual policies based on these standards.
- In accordance with the CAEL standards, credit is awarded based on the assessment of a student's learning (not experience alone) by trained experts who use established criteria for the assessment of learning.
- All criteria established for assessment should be available to students, advisors, and assessors.
- Further information on CAEL's standards can be found on the CAEL Web site, http://www.cael.org.

## NEXT STEPS

1. Locate and review the policies and procedures for prior learning assessment at your college. Compare the school's policies to the CAEL standards.
2. Case Study: FAKEU!

As you know, CAEL is a national nonprofit organization that creates and manages effective learning strategies for working adults through partnerships with employers, higher education, the public sector, and labor.

The CAEL standards for assessing credit are important for the assessment of prior learning since there are many false providers. Look at the CAEL standards in this chapter and compare them to the following advertisement for credit for learning below. It's a fake advertisement, but unfortunately, there are "diploma mills," or false companies, like this one!

Advertisement: FakeU's New Service!

FakeU now offers degrees for sale. E-mail us your résumé, and we'll look at ALL your lifelong experience. We'll tell you if you have learned the equivalent of a college degree! We don't care about your goal or previously earned credit. Our trained customer service reps will assess the credit for you. The free phone assessment process only takes about 10 minutes. After we look at your résumé, you will send us a payment of $99.49 to receive your diploma in the mail. The process will save you four years' time on average, and $140,000 in tuition. Cash in on your experience now!

Clearly, FakeU does not follow the ten standards set forth by CAEL. But which standards does it specifically violate? Can you explain how?

For further study of prior learning assessment practices in the U.S., examine the online PDF of CAEL's study "Fueling the Race to Postsecondary Success: A 48-Institution Study of Prior Learning Assessment and Adult Student Outcomes" at http://www.cael.org/pdf/PLA_Fueling-the-Race.pdf. You can also read the article "The 'Prior Learning' Edge" at http://www.insidehighered.com/news/2010/03/01/prior from the March 1, 2010 edition of *Inside Higher Ed* for a review of the report.

Name one of the findings from the CAEL report. Why do you think the finding is important?

# PART

# II

# Transcripts and Testing

# Evaluation of Transcripts and Training

## CHAPTER 5

## What Does This Chapter Cover and Why?

This chapter provides an overview of obtaining transcripts and training, including:

- Transcripts of college credit from colleges or universities (full- or part-time)
- Transcripts of military service and education
- Transcripts by ACE
- Training or examination records not certified by ACE

Obtaining transcripts of previous college work, military experience, certifications, or training is one of the first steps in the educational planning process.

## What Are College Course Transcripts and How Do I Request Official Copies?

A college transcript is an official document from a college that lists the names and dates of courses taken, grades received, overall **grade point average**, and number of credits earned. Students should obtain official transcripts from previous college work as early as possible to start the **admissions** process (see Box 5.1). Some students make their decision to attend the college that accepts the most transfer credit, but that should just be one consideration when choosing the right institution.

It is important to obtain transcripts from every college attended, even if the transcript shows several bad grades. As part of the transcription process, the college reviews the records and considers only the courses that meet the college's specific standards for transfer credit. Additionally, some colleges transfer the credits earned but not the grades. In any case, often past behavior is not a predictor of future success in college, especially with adult learners.

## BOX 5.1    Official and Unofficial Copies of Transcripts

Colleges require that transcripts be sent directly from one institution to the other in order to verify accuracy of the information.

Official transcripts—transcripts sent directly from one college to another with the official seal of the institution. Some colleges can send electronic copies of an official transcript directly to another college's registrar or admissions office (not a student), but the electronic copy will always be followed by a mailed paper copy.
Unofficial transcripts—working copies of your records that do not have the official seal stamped on the document and are often used to help students determine plans during the initial phases of the admission process. The unofficial transcript is also known as a worksheet.
Some colleges allow you to request an unofficial copy of your transcript online through a transcript ordering center (fee required), while others require either a personal visit to the registrar's office or a written request.
Note: If you have been dismissed from a college or university for unsatisfactory performance, that action should not prevent the college from sending an official transcript to another institution. However, if you are in financial arrears with the college, it is doubtful the registrar will send a transcript until financial arrangements have been made.

Students can obtain instructions for transcript requests on the school's Web site or call the registrar's office. The instructions vary, but generally a request must include dates of attendance, former names (e.g., if you have taken a different or married name), address(es) where copies should be sent, and Social Security number or student identification number. Transcript fees are low in cost—generally less than $10—and must be included with the request. Carefully following the instructions to request transcripts will help avoid delays.

# What Is Accreditation and How Does It Affect Transfer Agreements?

"Accreditation" is a term used to reflect the status granted to an educational institution that has met or exceeded certain criteria. It is a rigorous "seal of approval" that ensures the quality of an institution or degree program. Transfer of credit from one college to another is often dependent upon accreditation standards. The standard applies to the accreditation that the college held at the time that a student attended. For U.S. schools, accreditation is recognized by the **Council for Higher Education Accreditation (CHEA)**, which has six regional accrediting bodies (see Appendix 3 on U.S. and international accrediting bodies). Regional accreditation helps facilitate the transfer of credits from one institution to another.

There are other accrediting bodies, such as the **Distance Education and Training Council (DETC)**; however, DETC accreditations are not as widely accepted as the regional accreditation. Colleges may review programs and develop internal agreements called **articulation agreements** or seamless transfer agreements that state how the credits will be accepted. The general rule is that **accredited institutions** are more likely to accept credit from other similarly accredited institutions. Likewise, non-accredited institutions are more likely to accept credit from other non-accredited institutions. Even if a college is not regionally accredited, it may have high standards and offer excellent instruction. Accreditation may be an issue if students are considering transferring courses or doing graduate work.

# How Much College Credit Will Transfer to My New Program?

Accreditation does not automatically guarantee the acceptance of transfer credit. The amount of credit transferred depends on the college's transfer policies, which may consider things like the type of degree, major, number of credits earned, and age of the credit (see Box 5.2). Some fields and subject matters like nursing require that the learning be relatively current, so the age of the credit may be a factor.

Transfer credit rules are complex, so students must work closely with the academic advisor at the college who makes the official determination. Often, students who are denied transfer credit because the college they attended did not meet accreditation standards use the portfolio method to earn credit.

## BOX 5.2  Transfer Credit

Students are more likely to receive transfer credits for credit that is:

- "C minus" or better grades. Rarely, colleges allow a limited number of "D" grades. Credit for courses you failed or did not complete will not transfer.
- 100 level or higher (college level). Credit for upper-division courses is transferred as upper-division (normally, 300–400 level) credit. Courses with a number less than 100 are considered developmental, or remedial, and do not count toward graduation.
- In areas needed to complete the degree or certificate.
- Not duplicated.
- Considered academic level; technical or specialized coursework may be transferred only as electives, or it may be restricted or denied.
- Acquired from a regionally accredited college.

Note: Credit that was earned in quarter hours, if needed, will be converted to **semester hours** (or vice versa).

# What Is a Diploma Mill or an Accreditation Mill?

The Council for Higher Education Accreditation (CHEA) warns that diploma mills are "dubious providers of educational offerings or operations that offer certificates and degrees that may be considered bogus. [Students] may also encounter '**accreditation mills**' which are dubious providers of accreditation and quality assurance or operations that offer a certification of quality of institutions without a proper basis" ("Important Questions," 2011).

Both terms represent quick fixes, or an easy way to obtain a degree with little concern about mastery of knowledge, skills, or abilities. CHEA provides a list of questions to help individuals identify diploma or accreditation mills (see http://www.chea.org/pdf/fact_sheet_6_diploma_mills.pdf).

# How Do I Obtain International Transcripts?

United States colleges welcome international students to their campuses and distance education programs, but the transcript evaluation may take longer to complete. Some colleges complete their own evaluation of transcripts from foreign countries using published guidelines from such sources as the Council on International Educational Exchange. Most colleges require students to have their transcripts evaluated by a private organization because of the difficulty involved in assessing the titles, grades, and course levels. Students should select the agency recommended by the college they plan to attend and expect to pay for the service. Once the credential evaluation is received from the private organization, a college will make its own decision regarding transfer credit.

## Can I Appeal a Transcript Decision?

Colleges have guidelines for appeals if a student thinks that the decision made regarding transferability or placement of a specific course should be reconsidered. Sometimes supplying additional information such as course descriptions, letters from other colleges that have accepted the credit, or course syllabi can be useful for appealing a decision. However, students should understand that policies are set by colleges so that every student's credit is assessed fairly, and there may be valid reasons for not transferring credit. Students may want to find out how the decision was made before going through a time-consuming appeals process. In cases where transfer credit is denied due to failure to meet accreditation standards, prior learning assessment can be the best option to gain credit when a student's learning is college level.

## How Do I Obtain Transcripts for Military Service and Training?

The American Council on Education, a private organization, has evaluated military occupations and training courses for academic credit since 1945. Credit recommendations are published in the ACE *Guide to the Evaluation of Educational Experiences in the Armed Services* (a reference tool used by college administrators). Military training, education, courses, and occupational specialties can be evaluated for college credit. For instance, according to ACE (2011), the average number of academic credits awarded from an Army AARTS transcript is 14 semester hours.

Students should start by obtaining their military records (Military DD-214) or training records (DD295 forms). If a copy of the discharge paper is unavailable, students can request one from the branch of the military in which they served. The ACE Military Program evaluates courses provided through the Air Force, Army, Coast Guard, Department of Defense, Navy, and Marines. Credit recommendations for military occupations are based on the skills, competencies, and knowledge gained. ACE has simplified the process of assigning course recommendations by providing transcripts of military records and education. The ACE Web site provides a searchable course and occupation list.

After obtaining transcripts, if the record is incomplete, students should make requests for changes directly to the branch of the military in which they served. When a college receives the necessary official documentation, it will make the final credit determinations. Refer to Appendix 4 for specific information about how to obtain military transcripts.

## How Do I Find Information on ACE Recommendations for Training, Certifications, and Professional Examination?

In addition to evaluating military credit, ACE offers a college credit recommendation service that evaluates training courses sponsored by professional and nonprofit organizations, labor unions, Fortune 500 corporations, the government, hospitals, businesses, and industry. In addition to evaluating training and certifications, ACE provides college credit recommendations for passing professional examinations. ACE conducts assessments by evaluating the content, textbooks, level of instruction, classroom procedures, and expertise of the instructors. Credit recommendations are published in the ACE *National Guide to Educational Credit for Training Programs*, a reference guide used by college administrators. The ACE national guide also provides a searchable list of the training programs, certifications, and examinations that have been evaluated. You can access the guide at www.acenet.edu/nationalguide. Students who find that the training certification or exam they've passed has been evaluated can follow the directions on the Web site to download a request for an official ACE transcript.

## What Types of Training Does ACE Recommend?

Box 5.3 shows a brief sampling of the training providers, credentials, and exams reviewed by ACE as listed on their Web site. Students should check the site frequently to see if ACE has added any new examinations or suppliers of training.

## Does a College Always Follow the ACE Recommendations for Credit?

No, ACE only makes credit recommendations. The recommendations state the academic level, such as vocational, lower division, upper division, or graduate, as well as recommended semester hours.

## BOX 5.3  Sample Training Providers and ACE Recommendations

| TRAINING PROVIDERS EVALUATED | CERTIFICATIONS AND EXAMS |
|---|---|
| AT&T | The Association for Legal |
| Learning Tree International | Professionals |
| Lucent Technologies, Inc. | Certified Computer Programmer |
| McDonald's Corporation | Certified Novell Administrator |
| Microsoft Corporation | Certified Professional Secretary |
| Montessori Associates | Certified Purchasing Manager |
| Mortgage Bankers Association | Chartered Financial Consultant |
| of America | FAA Pilot, Engineer, Mechanic |
| New Horizons Computer Learning | Licenses |
| Centers, Inc. | Microsoft Office Specialist |
| PADI International, Inc. | Respiratory Therapy Technician |
| Program National Inst. for | |
| Automotive Service Excellence | |
| Starbucks | |
| U.S. Postal Service | |
| Verizon Communications | |
| Walt Disney Co. | |

Once ACE makes a recommendation, colleges have three options:

1. Accept the ACE credit recommendations
2. Reject the ACE credit recommendations
3. Accept the ACE credit recommendations with adjustments or changes

# What If My Training, Certification, or Exam Has Not Been Reviewed by ACE?

In addition to ACE-approved credit designations, some colleges accept national or state licenses such as real estate licenses, aviation licenses, and professional health certifications. Some colleges have investigated training programs and developed articulation agreements that detail how credits will be recognized at their school. If the program has not been evaluated by the college, students may have the option to petition for credit by writing a formal request with attached documentation. Even if the training is ACE certified, the college may ask for a more detailed explanation to make a credit determination. Box 5.4 shows a sample request for credit based on training. However, students should always follow the requirements of the institution they are attending.

## BOX 5.4 Sample Training Evaluation Request

**Petition for Credit Based on Training, Certification, or Examinations**

**Contact information:** Name, address, phone number, e-mail, student identification number

**Type of degree sought:** Attach copies of planned coursework (degree plan) and official or unofficial copies of transcripts, if available.

**Title of training:** Sponsoring institution that provided the instruction. Dates and hours of training.

Describe each training experience and the learning that you acquired from the training. Attach supporting documentation such as certificates, human resource records, course description, outline of the content, letter of verification, or instructor qualifications.

Is the training or exam ACE recommended? (Yes or no.) If yes, attach a copy of the ACE recommendation.

**Pre-training experience and preparation:** List relevant knowledge and skills that you acquired before the training (include dates and names of organizations where you gained the knowledge, skills, and abilities). Describe any preparation you did before attending the training.

**Training and learning:** Describe the specific knowledge, skills, and abilities that you gained from the course. If used, describe or show the results of the training's evaluation method. Attach records or documents that verify the level of training and learning.

**Post-training application of the learning:** Describe how and where you applied what you learned. Describe the level of learning that you acquired.

**Verification clause and signature:**
I attest that the information provided and documents are a true and accurate description of training that I have received.

Signed _____  Dated _____

## If My Training or Certifications Are Not Evaluated, What Other Methods Can I Use to Earn Credit?

Training records and certificates make excellent supporting documentation for building a portfolio for credit (see Chapter 11 on supporting documentation). Or, a student may use his or her knowledge to take a CLEP or challenge exam (see Chapter 6 on examinations).

# Adult Learner Profiles

In our adult learner profiles, we met Andrew, who earned credit from a Bible college, and Tim, who earned credit through a technical college. Due to accreditation standards, they were not able to transfer these credits directly; however, both students were able to successfully petition for credit through the portfolio method.

In addition, Tim was able to receive one credit for a Microsoft Office Specialist certification because the college he attended accepted the ACE-reviewed recommendations. Chris plans on requesting credit recommendations for her military service through ACE when she enrolls in college next fall. Maria, however, had certifications that were not ACE reviewed.

Maria had obtained a CPR and first aid certification through the American Montessori Society while applying for her day care license. When she was running her day care, she used her skills to assist children with minor injuries, even aiding a child who fell off a swing set and was seriously hurt. Maria used the training request form to obtain one credit in first aid toward her degree program.

## REVIEW

- Requests for official copies of transcripts should be sent as early as possible in the admissions process.

- ACE provides college credit recommendations for professional training, certifications, and exams as well as military service and education.

- Colleges have the final decision about how many transfer credits are accepted and how they are applied.

## NEXT STEPS

1. Review your learning inventory created in Next Steps Exercise 1.1. Request transcripts based on your previous college, training, or military service.

2. Consider what prior learning assessment methods (such as testing or portfolio) could be used to demonstrate areas of knowledge and learning that are not accepted through transcript or training evaluation.

## ADDITIONAL RESOURCES

American Council on Education College Credit Recommendation Service @ http://www.acenet.edu/

Council on Higher Education Accreditation (CHEA) @ www.chea.org

This Web site lists the United States Regional Accreditation Associations

## CHAPTER 6

# Credit by Examination

## What Some Students Have Said about Earning College Credit by Examination

*"Test taking was a great way to fulfill credits while I was traveling extensively for my job. I was able to earn 18 credits in three months' time."*

*"I highly recommend testing but it takes discipline to prepare. I passed 11 CLEP and DSST tests. I found lots of study guide material for the CLEP tests, and my ability to carefully read the test questions improved after each test I took."*

*"I took a challenge exam (at the college) to waive the lower-level course requirement for my computer science degree. Passing the exam allowed me to enroll in the next level of programming courses."*

—SUCCESSFUL ADULT LEARNERS

## What Types of Exams Exist?

Four types of exams will be described in this chapter. Upon entering college, the student will first be introduced to entrance exams and placement exams. A second set of exams includes college-specific course challenge exams and standardized national exams.

### Entrance Exams

Entrance exams are exams that some colleges require for admissions. However, many colleges that offer undergraduate-level courses to adult professionals do not require these students to take entrance exams. Some colleges may require students to take an English-language exam that measures their ability to use and understand English, such as the **TOEFL**®.

## Placement Exams

Placement exams are often required by United States colleges. These exams are used to help students determine what level of classes to take first. The most common placement exams are in English and mathematics. Placement exams are not admissions tests that impact a student's acceptance. Instead, the exams help students to determine the appropriate level of learning they need before they enroll in a course that may be too difficult or too easy to complete.

## College-specific Course Challenges

**Course challenges**, also known as exams for waiver or challenge exams, are offered by some colleges. Normally these exams are written and scored by the college's instructors and are based on the final exam for the course. Consult the testing center or an academic advisor for more information about challenge exams.

## Standardized National Exams

Standardized national exams are intended to test general knowledge in areas such as history, languages, art, science, and English, which are subjects required for most two- and four-year degrees. Standardized exams are written by professional testing companies or private universities and are administered in licensed testing sites throughout the country. The most common standardized tests that measure experiential learning are the College Level Exam Program (CLEP) and DSST (formerly **DANTES** or the DANTES Subject Standardized Tests, originally designed for the military). Box 6.1 shows a sampling of some of the CLEP and DSST exams available as listed on their Web sites at http://www.collegeboard.com and http://www.getcollegecredit.com, respectively.

Some colleges—such as Thomas Edison State College, Excelsior College, and Ohio University—allow students outside their institution to take exams they have created. In addition, national organizations, such as the National League for Nursing (NLN), offer challenge exams that can be taken at certified testing centers. See the list of additional resources at the end of this chapter for Web sites and information on each of these exams.

# BOX 6.1   Sample CLEP and DSST Exam Titles

## CLEP EXAM TITLES

### Humanities
American Literature
Analyzing and Interpreting
  Literature
English Composition
College Composition
College Composition Modular
English Literature
Humanities
Foreign Languages
French Language (Levels 1 and 2)
German Language (Levels 1 and 2)
Spanish Language (Levels 1 and 2)
American Government
Human Growth and Development
Introduction to Educational
  Psychology
Principles of Macroeconomics
Principles of Microeconomics
Introductory Psychology
Introductory Sociology

### Social Sciences and History
U.S. History I: Early Colonization
  to 1877
U.S. History II: 1865 to the Present
Western Civilization I: Ancient Near
  East to 1648
Western Civilization II: 1648 to the
  Present

### Science and Mathematics
Precalculus
Calculus
College Algebra
College Mathematics
Biology
Chemistry
Natural Sciences

### Business
Information Systems and Computer
  Applications
Principles of Management
Financial Accounting
Introductory Business Law
Principles of Marketing

## DSST EXAM TITLES

### Humanities and Technology
Ethics in America
Introduction to World Religions
Principles of Public Speaking
Technical Writing

### Social Sciences and History
Art of the Western World
Western Europe since 1945
An Introduction to the Modern
  Middle East
Human/Cultural Geography
Rise and Fall of the Soviet Union
A History of the Vietnam War
The Civil War and Reconstruction
Foundations of Education
Lifespan Developmental Psychology
General Anthropology
Introduction to Law Enforcement
Criminal Justice
Fundamentals of Counseling
Substance Abuse

### Science and Mathematics
Astronomy
Here's to Your Health
Environment and Humanity
Fundamentals of College Algebra
Physical Geology
Principles of Physical Science I
Principles of Statistics

### Business
Principles of Finance
Principles of Financial Accounting
Human Resource Management
Organizational Behavior
Principles of Supervision
Business Law II
Introduction to Computing
Introduction to Business
Money and Banking
Personal Finance
Management Information
  Systems
Business Mathematics
Busness Ethics and Society

# What Are the Advantages of Using Credit by Examination?

Earning credit by exam is a high-yield and low-risk option for students who have knowledge in such areas as mathematics, humanities, foreign languages, business, science, and history. Test taking has several advantages. It is a convenient option for busy working adults who want to earn credits for learning or make up for missed courses. Test taking is an inexpensive option because many standardized exams cost around $100 for the equivalent of a three-credit course, which leaves students with more money to pay for coursework.

Students do risk losing the exam fees if they fail the exam, but failing a standardized national exam does not affect a student's grade point average. However, failing a college-specific course challenge may have heavier consequences. Overall, for many adult students who have the learning, the benefits of test taking outweigh the risks.

## What Exams Will the College Accept?

As with other assessment methods, there are no ironclad rules. Each college sets policies on the types of tests and credit recommendations they allow.

You may find that the college accepts credit for a CLEP exam in College Composition but not in American Government. Or perhaps within the college, the Division of Continuing Studies may award credit for many of the DSST exams, but the School of Business may not. As always, it is critical that you work with an advisor to take advantage of the available options at your college.

## What Are Some Types of Challenge Exams Offered by Colleges?

1. **Final exams or comprehensive exams** can be multiple choice, short answer, essay, or a combination, and may be based on lecture content and textbooks used for a specific course. Reading lists and course syllabi may be useful for studying.

2. **Demonstrations** allow students to actively exhibit their specific skills critical for competence, like a clinical nursing competency or a mechanical skill. The evaluator may give background on the demonstration beforehand so that the student can understand the context before completing the demonstration.

3. **Simulations** are used to replicate certain conditions that a student might encounter. Computer simulations may be used if creating the actual situation would take too much time or effort to set up. For example, a student might demonstrate competencies in a range of computer software skills by taking a computer-generated competency test. Or an electronics department may have a computer-aided circuit simulation.

4. **Case studies** give students an opportunity to apply a skill set to specific circumstances. For example, a student might be given a **case study** that describes a company's marketing challenges and then be asked to analyze the problem and present a solution. Students may be allowed time to complete a project, such as to design a marketing campaign based on the case study.

5. **Interviews or oral presentations** with one evaluator or a panel may be required alone or in combination with an exam or portfolio. Interviews are opportunities for students to address specifics about their prior learning (see Box 8.5 on portfolio interview preparation). Or a student may be asked to prepare an oral presentation to challenge a speech requirement.

## How Do National Standardized Exams and College-Specific Challenge Exams Compare?

To get an idea of how national standardized exams and college-specific challenge exams compare, Box 6.2 looks at CLEP and DSST exams (the two most common types of national standardized examinations) alongside challenge exams. Box 6.3 provides guidelines for challenge exam preparation.

## What Steps Are Involved in Earning Credit by Examination?

1. Check the policies regarding credit by examination at the college or nearest test site before taking any exam. Policy statements may be in a catalog, student handbook, or Web site under a heading such as testing, CLEP, credit by exam, advanced standing, advanced placement, adult learning, or prior learning assessment. Students who are close to graduating should check the deadline for accepting credit by examination.

2. Double check that the exam is acceptable for the credit needed. Unfortunately, students sometimes jump ahead and taken a test before verifying that the credit is acceptable, often resulting in a loss of both

# BOX 6.2 Comparison of National and College-Specific Exams

|  | NATIONAL STANDARDIZED EXAMS | COLLEGE-SPECIFIC COURSE CHALLENGES |
|---|---|---|
| Web sites | CLEP: http://www.college board.com<br>DSST: http://www.get collegecredit.com | See the individual college's Web site. |
| Description | Exams written by national companies that are tested and normed by experts. | Exams written by instructors or obtained by the college to determine student competencies based on a school's course offerings. |
| Scoring and credit assignment | Score recommendations are published; however, each college determines whether to follow the recommendations. | The college determines the acceptable grade and credit assignment. In some cases, course challenges are used to waive a required course. |
| Type | Primarily multiple choice. The CLEP College Composition exam requires an essay. | Varies (see Box 6.3). Exam may require a take-home portion. An interview with a faculty member may be required. |
| Cost | Nonrefundable. Less than $100 for three-credit-hour exams. | Nonrefundable. Cost varies. |
| Timed | CLEP: 90 minutes.<br>DSST: Up to two hours. | Timed or untimed, depending on the exam. |
| Where offered | Authorized testing centers throughout the country. See Web sites for information. | Offered only at the college in a testing center or computer lab. |
| Retake policy | Students can retake the exams after six months. | Normally, no retake allowed. |
| Study guides | CLEP: Exam description on Web site. Exam guides require a fee.<br>DSST: Web site has free practice exams and exam fact sheets.<br>Additional fee-based exam practice materials: Peterson's Practice Tests at | Study guides offered at the college. |

(continued)

| | NATIONAL STANDARDIZED EXAMS | COLLEGE-SPECIFIC COURSE CHALLENGES |
| --- | --- | --- |
| | http://www.petersons.com and REA Study Guide at http://www.rea.com/. | |
| Impact on grade point average | None. | May affect grade point average. See individual college's policies. |
| Transcript | Title of course and number of credits earned appear on transcript. | Title of course and number of credits earned appear on transcript. |
| | Credit may appear as credit by exam or transfer credit (distinguished from course credit) on the transcript. | Credit may or may not appear as credit by exam (distinguished from course credit) on the transcript. |

## BOX 6.3 Preparing for Challenge Exams

1. Students should find out as much information as possible about the competencies they will be asked to demonstrate as well as the setting and evaluation tools used. When guidelines are provided, students should review them several times and follow the requirements with attention to detail.
2. Students should try to replicate the demonstration, oral presentation, or simulation as closely as possible when preparing or practicing for the actual exam.
3. In some cases, students can preview the type of simulation equipment that is used, preview an exam question, or visit the room where the test is conducted. Visualizing the room in advance can help decrease testing anxiety. To ensure objectivity and fairness, students should not expect an in-depth conversation about the exam with the evaluator.

time and money. Never assume, for instance, that a test will satisfy a foundational course in the major. It is easy to be deceived by looking at the title alone, but many factors go into the assessment of whether a standardized exam is the equivalent of a course, including subject, lower or upper division, and a student's course record. As this book has stated frequently, always verify your selections.

3. Select the exam that best matches your learning. Some students must choose one of several options, such as exams that will satisfy humanities credit. The best way to determine which exam is most suitable for you is to take several practice tests and select the one in which you excelled. "Don't try to test out of something that is totally foreign to you," says Mary Martin, a college advisor. The exams test both general knowledge and the application of that knowledge to different contexts.

4. Schedule the exam date at a testing center. Some testing centers will be on campus and others won't. Find the testing center that is most convenient for you. Lists of authorized test centers that administer CLEP and DSST exams are published on their Web sites. If you are currently serving in the military in the U.S. or overseas, there is the option of taking DSST tests on military bases. You might schedule a time to visit the testing center to determine parking availability before your test day or arrange to view a sample CLEP test question on the computer screen and get more familiar with the forward and back buttons.

5. Obtain results. Generally, results are mailed to the student and to the college that is indicated on the test score form. Most CLEP results are available immediately on the testing computer. Some exams, such as College Composition, require written essays, and the results may take several weeks. The required score for earning the credit varies from exam to exam, so make sure to check the college's minimum passing score for the exam.

## What Information Can I Obtain from the Testing Center?

Testing centers have information on scheduling, fees, and registration. It is best to schedule a test at least several weeks in advance to guarantee a spot. Since the CLEP test is administered on a computer, there may be a limit on seating depending on the number of terminals available. Fees may be charged for changing or canceling a test date. The staff at the testing center can answer questions regarding time limits, check-in, form of identification needed, when to expect results, and retesting (if allowed). In addition, the testing center can provide information on accessibility and can make accommodations for those with a documented disability as set forth by the Americans with Disabilities Act (ADA).

Cell phone use and electronic devices are prohibited. You will be asked to place personal items and electronics in a locker. If secured lockers are not available, plan ahead to avoid bringing these items into the testing center. If calculators are allowed, the testing center will provide them.

# What Are Some Effective Ways to Review for an Exam?

When preparing to take an exam, it is important to review both content and test-taking strategies. The goal is that when a test taker walks into the exam room, she or he is as well prepared as possible to receive a passing score.

1. Review the study guides carefully. Take more than one practice test, if available, and closely examine the results.

2. Check libraries for study guides and reference books. When checking out guides from the library, be courteous of others and don't mark up the practice tests. CLEP and DSST exam guides provide lists of general reference books. Study guides for national exams do not list a specific book that a student can study to pass the exam, since the exams are based on prior learning. On the other hand, college-specific challenge exams are based on the textbooks for the course, so reviewing the texts can be beneficial. Many colleges make the course modules or syllabi available to help students determine the textbook used and topics covered.

3. Spend time studying your areas of weakness. It is not always productive to spend equal studying time on each part of the exam. A better strategy is to determine which areas are strengths and then focus on the weaknesses.

4. Study key words and concepts. Be prepared to apply knowledge, concepts, and theories to different situations and real-life issues.

# What Are Some Test-Taking Strategies?

1. Use your first guess. Research has shown that a first guess is often the correct response.

2. Determine if there is a penalty for guessing. If there is no penalty for guessing, mark an answer for every question.

3. Practice identifying words often used in multiple choice questions and learn how they can affect your answer. For example, qualifiers like *best, worst, always, never, all, most, some,* and *none* can completely alter the meaning of a statement. Likewise, the use of negatives, such as *no, none,* and *not,* and prefixes like *il-,* as in *illogical; un-,* as in *uninterested;* and *im-,* as in *impatient* can be misleading.

4. Create questions and answers if there are no practice questions.

5. Set blocks of time to study between work and family schedules. Short periods are more productive for memorizing than long stretches.

6. Collect study material in a separate briefcase in order to study on breaks during the workday.

7. Seize your most alert times of the day for learning (e.g., early morning or late at night) even if it is only for a 10- to 20-minute period.

8. Remember with intention. Motivation to remember makes the mind receptive to learning.

9. Anchor the learning with ideas and experience previously learned.

10. Explore a combination of methods to make studying an active, not a passive, process.

## What Strategies Can I Use to Study Based on My Learning Preference?

Learning styles are preferences or approaches that describe how a person learns best. Most learners have a combination of learning style preferences, but one or two may be strongest. Students can use their learning style strengths or a mix of learning styles to keep the process of studying active. Box 6.4 provides strategies for studying that match visual, auditory, and kinesthetic preferences. An online study resource that may be helpful is shown in Box 6.5.

### BOX 6.4   Test-Taking Strategies by Learning Style Preference

**Visual learners:** tend to learn through seeing or visualizing

- Study visual materials such as pictures, charts, maps, photos, and photographs
- Use colors to highlight or underline key words (avoid over-high-lighting)
- Visualize the concepts as pictures to assist memorization
- Illustrate ideas as pictures
- Create timelines for studying dates and add comment boxes
- Use mind-mapping software or create mind maps with drawing tools
- Write cartoons with bubbles to illustrate ideas

(continued)

- Use multimedia software such as PowerPoint to design a slide show
- Watch videos on the topic
- Study in a quiet place
- Skim through reading material to get a rough idea of what it is about before settling down to read it in detail (effective for all learning styles)
- Consider downloading e-books to your computer or a mobile device
- Create a blog, Web site, Prezi presentation (see http://www.prezi. com), or document site of key terms, articles, and links to valuable resources

**Auditory learners:** tend to learn through listening

- Talk to friends and family members about the subject area
- Participate in community discussions on the topic such as a lecture on art history at a museum
- Prepare a speech on the topic for a public speaking class or for a Toastmasters club
- Read the practice questions and answers out loud
- Use a tape recorder to record notes
- Use some creativity to create a song, advertisement, jingle, or mnemonic device
- Create and tell a story that demonstrates an application of the concept
- Watch a video on the topic with another person and discuss the contents
- Listen to audio tapes on the topic while driving and talk back to them
- Brush up on a foreign language by listening to foreign language radio or television stations or hanging out in a store, coffee shop, or restaurant where the language is frequently spoken

**Tactile or kinesthetic learners:** tend to learn by doing something, moving, and touching

- Walk or pace slowly while studying
- Read while on treadmill or exercise bike
- Squeeze a ball while reading
- Use modeling clay to create a representation of a concept
- Work standing up
- Create flashcards in multiple colors and study the flashcards in groups of three

(continued)

- Set short blocks of time to study and then move around
- Stretch muscles and move legs or arms while studying
- Use the same music in the background during every study period
- Find free Web Resources and play simulations and games on the topic (Merlot.org provides navigational links by subject matter and reviews free multimedia educational resources on the Web)
- Purchase practice tests, if available, in an online or CD-ROM format (DSST has an iStudySmart resource that allows students to take in-depth study courses online)

## Is Test-Taking Anxiety Normal?

Absolutely. A level of test-taking nervousness is normal and very common. Many adult learners have been out of the classroom for a decade or more, so they may have little confidence in their test-taking ability. The anxiety may be due to any number of factors, including negative past experiences, a feeling of unpreparedness, or inexperience. Even though the anxiety may be uncomfortable, a small amount should not prevent students from trying this option. Students who feel paralyzed by test-taking anxiety may consider using the portfolio method to earn credit. However, there are a number of strategies that may be helpful for reducing testing anxiety, so conducting research on the Internet or in books or taking study skills courses can help you find and experiment with stress-reduction methods. Certainly, adequate preparation is one of the best methods of reducing test-taking anxiety.

### Box 6.5 Khan Academy: A Free Self-Paced Study Resource

Sal Khan started out creating math videos for his cousins and posting them on YouTube.com. Now, Khan Academy (http://www.khanacademy.org/) has grown into a nonprofit organization that provides lessons in college algebra, physics, finance, history, and other topics. Self-paced exercises and assessments are also available on the site.

Sal Khan has an amazing gift for breaking down concepts into small bites of learning and delivering the ideas using a tablet and a conversational tone. The videos can help students fill gaps in their learning and prepare them for exams and college courses. After accessing the site, use the search box to find general areas of learning, such as Algebra, or specific lessons, such as Histograms.

# REVIEW

- Obtaining credit by examination can be a low-risk, low-cost, and high-yield way to earn college credit.
- Check the policies on credit by examination before registering and paying for an exam.
- Optimally, study both test-taking techniques and test content.
- Exams measure experiential learning, so students should choose tests that closely match their knowledge and experience.
- Maximize studying time by concentrating on areas of weakness and experimenting with a variety of active study techniques.
- Combining both testing and portfolio assessment helps students earn credits in more areas than assessment using just one PLA method.

# NEXT STEPS

1. Identify areas for which you may be able to take an exam. Navigate the CLEP and DSST Web sites for additional information, and then speak with your advisor for more ideas and guidance.

2. Create a list of action items with a timeline for studying and taking an exam. Start with the exam date and fill in blocks of time to research, review, and take practice exams. Or use time-management software or a calendar to record the deadlines.

3. Visit the testing center, if possible. Arrange for a quick tour of the facility. Prepare a list of questions before the visit and interview the testing staff.

4. Write or explain the pros and cons of using credit by exam for foundational courses.

5. Find useful Web sites or interview a student or students who have used the credit-by-exam method. What tips did they offer?

6. Determine the best study strategies based on experimentation.

7. Find resources on handling test anxiety and try one or two tips.

8. Research study materials such as books, videos, and audio recordings that will help in preparation for an exam. Many colleges and some local public libraries can assist students in borrowing material from other institutions.

# ADDITIONAL RESOURCES

Exams

College-Level Examination Program (CLEP) @ http://www.collegeboard.com/
student/testing/clep/about.html
> Here you will find information on CLEP exams, what they are, and how to
> take them. Study guides are available for a fee.

The ACE National Guide to College Credit for Workforce Training @ http://
www2.acenet.edu/credit/?page=about
> Use this site to see an A–Z list of organizations who offer training pro-
> grams that can be evaluated for college credit.

DSST Credit by Exam Program @ http://www.getcollegecredit.com
> DSST offers exams in 38 subjects. On the Web site, you can download
> individual study sheet PDFs for their exams.

Education Testing Service @ http://www.ets.org

The Education Testing Service has information on the TOEFL and GRE exams.
> Nursing Challenge Exams @ http://www.nln.org

Advanced Placement Examinations (AP Exams) @ http://www.collegeboard.com/
student/testing/ap/about.html

Thomas Edison State College Examination Program (TECEP) @ http://www.tesc.
edu/701.php Both the TECEP and the Excelsior and Ohio exams below are more
specialized and are not used as much as the programs listed above.

Excelsior College Examinations (ECE) @ http://www.excelsior.edu/ecapps/exams/
creditByExam.jsf?gw=1

Ohio University Exams @ http://www.ohio.edu/independent.


OpenCourseWare

OpenCourseWare (OCW) Web sites provide instructional materials for free.
Sites may include lecture notes, images, podcasts, and multimedia content.
Explore the Web sites below and see what you can find for your own course of
study.

OCW Finder @ http://www.opencontent.org/ocwfinder

The World's 50 Best Open Courseware Collections @ http://onlineuniversity
rankings.org/2009/the-worlds-50-best-open-courseware-collections

Massachusetts Institute of Technology OCW @ http://ocw.mit.edu/index.htm

The Open University's LearningSpace @ http://openlearn.open.ac.uk

Kaplan University OCW @ http://ocw.kaplan.edu

Multimedia Educational Research for Learning and Online Teaching @ http://
www.merlot.org

Khan Academy @ http://www.khanacademy.org


Google Scholar

Supplement your knowledge further with Google Scholar at http://scholar.
google.com/. Enter a search term to find summaries, also known as abstracts,
of scholarly articles on your subject. Some abstracts will have links to the full
article; others might not. However, if you are a current student, you may be
able to configure Google Scholar to link to your college's proprietary databases of articles. Contact the library staff at the college where you are enrolled
to find out.

Fee-Based Study Materials
Peterson's Practice Tests @ http://www.petersons.com
REA Study Guide @ http://www.rea.com
Online courses to study for CLEP, DSST, and ECE tests @ http://www.iStudySmart.com

# PART

# III

# Portfolio
# Development

## CHAPTER 7

# Learning Theory and Application

*"You do not really understand something unless you can explain it to your grandmother."*

—ALBERT EINSTEIN

## Why Study Learning Principles?

As you are well aware by now, prior learning assessment emphasizes the fact that experience alone, such as the number of years on a job, does not solely determine the awarding of college credit. In fact, it is the learning garnered from that experience that is of the greatest import. In order to give you the tools you need to successfully discover and understand your own experiential learning, this chapter introduces some fundamental definitions and principles related to the concept of learning.

The process of unpacking learning is hard work because it requires recalling events. It also requires learners to carefully reflect on experiences and assess how the learning relates to college courses. As stated by Malcolm Knowles (1975), "Performance assessment in the area of understanding and insight requires that a participant demonstrate his ability to size up situations, see patterns, develop categories, figure out cause-and-effect relationships, and in general, to apply knowledge and thought processes to the analysis and solution of problems" (p. 87). Completing the exercises presented throughout this chapter will help you tap into the events that shaped your learning.

## What Is Experiential Learning?

Learning can involve one or more methods, including memorization, study, classroom instruction, observation, and hands-on experience. Experiential learning, however, involves direct participation in, or observation of, an event. Learning occurs when participants gain something, such as an understanding, appreciation, ability, or skill. According to Sheckley & Keeton, "Experience yields explicit knowledge only if reflected upon" (as cited in Fiddler et al., 2006, p. 5). Thus, experiential learning involves direct participation or observation plus the acquisition of knowledge, skills, and abilities.

Notice the strong nouns and verbs Luckner and Nadler (1997) use to describe the experience of active learning:

> *What is experience? It is an event, training, activity, occurrence, adventure, experience, endeavor, lecture, outing, undertaking, project, seminar, quest, escapade, happening, or effort. The experience is nothing more than a reference point or marker in one's life. It can be overlooked, discounted, passed by, ignored, or forgotten. Then again, it can be the turning point, catalyst, energizer, enzyme, breakthrough, impetus, stimulus, incentive, or driving force for great changes and learning . . . What we bring into it, take from it, leave there, reach for, and continue to use, [is] all up to us. (xv)*

Students who write about their experiential learning become more aware of future learning opportunities. In fact, they become mindful and purposeful about the learning experiences they encounter—they go looking for learning.

Learning occurs before, during, and after an event. Active learners approach situations by asking questions such as when, why, and how. In addition to learning how to learn and being more purposeful about learning, the process of writing and reflecting helps students become aware of the strengths and weaknesses in their learning style (see Box 7.1). After examin-

## BOX 7.1   Experiential Learning

1. Describe one of the following:
   - A time when you learned a skill by trial and error
   - A skill you learned that you applied to a new situation
2. Write a step-by-step page of instructions on how to do something, such as perform a computer function, play a sport, or operate a piece of equipment. What did you see, notice, observe, examine, watch, ponder, or think about when explaining your step-by-step process?
3. What are some ways you could become more deliberate about your learning?
4. What are the benefits of promoting a learning culture in an organization?

ing a business failure, one student stated, "If I ever start a business again, I will spend more time planning, researching, and finding the necessary amount of capital before I just jump in and launch my dream."

## In What Ways Are Adult Learners Unique?

The study of adult learning gained momentum when Malcolm Knowles (1984) recognized that adult learners differ from their younger counterparts in a number of significant ways. Knowles recognized that adults are self-directed learners. In addition, Knowles and others have observed that adults approach learning as problem solving and learn best when the topic is relevant to their life. As a result, prior learning experiences provide a rich basis for classroom discussion and learning. Moreover, adult learners personalize their learning, applying the strategies and principles learned in the classroom at work. Teaching techniques such as case studies and applications have proven to be particularly effective with adult learners. Accordingly, instructors become more like facilitators of students' learning rather than lecturers or "sages on the stage."

## What Are the Strengths and Challenges of Experiential Learning?

To answer this question, we must begin by identifying and describing the differences between experiential learning and traditional classroom learning. Certainly, learning in the traditional classroom environment has many advantages. Classroom learning benefits from an instructor who is dedicated to completing objectives that will help students learn the skills, theories, and concepts needed in a field. In addition, for hands-on learners, classroom environments are like laboratories where learning is practiced, and students benefit from the input of other learners.

There can be, however, some drawbacks to classroom learning. Many students cram for exams and forget the knowledge they've gained because it is not applicable to their experience. Also, while many students are familiar with the theories and ideas in a classroom, they may not be able to apply the concepts to real-life settings.

One strength of experiential learning is that students acquire their knowledge in the field, with the assistance of experts and by direct application. One of the drawbacks of experiential learning is that it is very difficult to measure. In addition, there may be gaps in the learning. In the way that a classroom-taught student has difficulty applying concepts to real-life situations, experiential learners are generally less aware of the theories, principles, and concepts that underlie their learning even as they may be using them in their workplace. Because of this disconnect, experiential learners may have a more difficult time transferring their learning to other contexts or even to the classroom.

The main difference between the two ways of learning has been described as input versus outcome (Coleman, 1976, pp. 49–61; Whitaker, 1989, p. 2). Since the sources of learning differ significantly, the learning processes and outcomes, although similar, look and feel different. For experiential learners, the process of learning, or the input, is through observation and doing, and the result, or outcome, is more inductive. That is, adults will observe and act in a number of situations and draw conclusions, sometimes unconsciously (see tacit knowledge below), based on their participation. In classroom learning, a more deductive process occurs in which students study conclusions from experts in the field (input) and then apply the concepts and theories to specific instances, such as case studies (Coleman, 1976).

When the comparison to classroom learning is applied to the assessment of prior learning, it becomes clearer why students who petition for credit based on experience may need to update their knowledge of the concepts that underlie their subject matter to make their learning more complete. To learn or update their learning on appropriate concepts and theories, students read books, talk with others, or get training. According to Whitaker (1989), when preparing the petition for credit, it is essential to leaven the mix of theory and practical application with ample portions of reflection: "The learning is not complete until the learner has some understanding of what both the theory and the practical experience mean. It isn't enough to have both in isolation; the learner needs to know why they are necessary [and] how each extends the value of the other" (p. 14). Ultimately, knowledge of relevant theoretical principles helps experiential learners understand how their learning fits into a larger context. Follow the steps in Box 7.2 to begin linking your theoretical knowledge to your practical experience.

## What Is Tacit Knowledge and How Does It Relate to Prior Learning?

Tacit knowledge is knowledge that we are largely unaware we are using—it can be a hunch, gut feeling, or response that thoughtfully draws from a large pool of knowledge. In *The Inquiring Organization*, Kikoski and Kikoski (2004) write, "It is possible that each one of us knows more than we can say, that each individual possesses a vast reservoir of personal knowledge—that is yet 'unsaid.' The 'unsaid' includes the entire background of one's experi-

## BOX 7.2   Linking Theoretical and Practical Experience

Survey the textbook that is required for a specific college course. Find several key concepts, terms, or theoretical models taught in the course. Key terms are often typed in a **bold-faced** font, and theoretical models are often illustrated in a graphic. If the course uses hands-on learning, locate several general rules of thumb that govern the subject matter. Or, navigate the tip database at http://tip.psychology.org. The site links to explanations of theories, learning domains, and learning concepts.

1. What theories or concepts did you find that closely match your practical experience or observations?
2. Does understanding the theories and concepts help extend the value of your practical experience? In what way?

ences, unarticulated assumption[s], and unconscious thoughts, as well as inferences drawn from them . . . What is 'unsaid' and 'unexpressed' could be the reservoirs of tacit knowledge. Tacit knowledge is the less familiar, unconventional form of knowledge . . . It is the knowledge of which we are not conscious, the knowledge that we cannot say. Tacit knowledge is the knowledge of which we are unaware, and unaware of using" (p. 66).

This tacit knowledge, or rich source of untapped knowledge, can be accessed by reflecting on events  (see Box 7.3). Further, reflecting on experiences is an ". . . active process of exploration and discovery which often leads to very unexpected outcomes" (Boud, Keogh, & Walker, 1985, p. 7). The process of understanding past events and assimilating new information stimulates the brain's reflective muscle. The brain makes connections with information, especially when that information is personally relevant. Drawing on tacit knowledge leads to new understanding and thus to new learning.

## BOX 7.3   Drawing from Tacit Knowledge

You have just been promoted to a supervisory or management position in your company. Drawing on your knowledge of organizations, describe two or three specific ways you could motivate your employees. Did the discovery of answers lead to insights that you had not previously considered?

The prior learning assessment process involves recalling past events. When students are involved in this level of reflection, new learning occurs.

## What Are Intelligences, and How Do They Affect Experiential Learning and PLA?

Howard Gardner is the John H. and Elisabeth A. Hobbs Professor of Cognition and Education at the Harvard Graduate School of Education, and he is what we might call the "father" of multiple intelligence theory. Gardner has received honorary degrees from 26 colleges and universities, and *Foreign Policy* and *Prospect* magazines named him as one of the 100 most influential public intellectuals in the world in 2005 and 2008.

Gardner first proposed his theory of **multiple intelligences** in 1983, being the first to posit that intelligence isn't bound to a single, general ability, but instead to a variety of aptitudes. His groundbreaking concept remains an important point of research and theory in the fields of education and psychology.

Most people find they have strengths in several of these aptitudes, or intelligences:

**Logical-mathematical intelligence** Consists of the ability to detect patterns, reason deductively, and think logically. This intelligence is most often associated with scientific and mathematical thinking.

**Linguistic intelligence** involves having a mastery of language. This intelligence includes the ability to effectively manipulate language to express oneself or to remember information.

**Spatial intelligence** gives one the ability to create and manipulate mental images in order to solve problems.

**Musical intelligence** encompasses the capability to recognize and compose musical pitches, tones, and rhythms.

**Body-kinesthetic intelligence** is the ability to use one's mental abilities to coordinate one's own bodily movements.

**Interpersonal intelligence** allows one to understand the feelings and intentions of others.

**Intrapersonal intelligence,** with *intra* meaning "inside a person," is the ability to understand one's own feelings and motivations.

**Naturalistic intelligence** is the ability to discern and see subtle patterns in nature.

**Spiritual/existential intelligence** is the ability to ponder questions about life, death, and ultimate realities. This intelligence is associated with the recognition of the spiritual.

Remember Box 6.4 that listed ways for visual learners, auditory learners, and kinesthetic learners to enhance their study techniques? Can you see the connections between learning preferences and multiple intelligences? When students uncover their prior learning, they often recognize threads in their abilities and preferred learning styles.

Another significance of multiple intelligence theory to experiential learning is found in Daniel Goleman's (2006) work *Emotional Intelligence: Why It Can Matter More Than IQ.*

Goleman recognized that high emotional IQ gives workers a competitive edge. Competencies in such areas as intrapersonal and interpersonal intelligence are often unrecognized, yet knowledge of self and the ability to work with others often leads to success in the workplace. Some of the personal and social competencies included in emotional IQ are self-awareness, self-motivation, persistence, empathy, and social skills. Answer the questions in Box 7.4 to begin exploring your intelligences and competencies.

## BOX 7.4   Multiple Intelligences and Emotional IQ

1. Describe a process or a skill that you had to learn in order to succeed in your job. What intelligences did you rely on the most? Least? For example, a student who solved a telecommunication problem might have used interpersonal intelligence to ask someone knowledgeable for help, linguistic intelligence to follow the verbal step-by-step instructions, and logical-mathematical intelligence to think through a program error.
2. Describe a workplace problem where you used intrapersonal and interpersonal intelligence to arrive at a solution.

# What Is Kolb's Cycle of Learning and How Can It Help Me Understand My Prior Learning?

David Kolb is a professor of organizational behavior at Case Western Reserve University's Weatherhead School of Management and the author of a multitude of books, chapters, and journal articles on experiential learning, learning styles, learning flexibility, and team learning. Kolb holds four honorary degrees for his contributions and research in experiential learning. His work has also garnered several awards, including CAEL's Morris T. Keeton Award in 1991; he and Alice Kolb received the Educational Pioneers Award from the National Society of Experiential Education in 2008. Most recently, he coauthored an entry to the 2011 *Oxford Handbook of Lifelong Learning* with colleague Angela Passarelli. In his influential book *Experiential Learning: Experience as the Source of Learning and Development* (1984), Kolb described learning as a cycle with four parts: concrete experience, reflection and observation, abstract conceptualization, and active experimentation. When each stage of the cycle is utilized, learning becomes more complete; likewise, when a portion is left out, the learning is shortchanged.

The cycle of learning proposed in Kolb's model shows how concrete experiences can lead to personal reflection on the experience. This reflection then leads to abstract conceptualization, which might manifest itself in a set of conclusions or rules of thumb derived from the experience as well as insight into applicable theories or other concepts. The conclusions reached next lead to ways of testing the new learning, what Kolb calls active experimentation, and then ultimately back to a new concrete experience.

The crux of Kolb's model is the step of reflection, an often neglected part of the learning process. In the book *Dimensions of Adult Learning* (2004), Foley encapsulates Kolb saying that for Kolb learning is a process "oscillating between concrete emotional experiences and deliberate cognitive reflection. Although all adults are exposed to a multitude of life experiences, Kolb maintains, not everyone learns from these. *Learning happens only when there is reflective thought and internal 'processing' by the learner*, in a way that actively makes sense of an experience and links it to previous learning" (p. 60, emphasis added).

Although Kolb first published his theory of experiential learning in 1984, his model remains an active catalyst for current discussions on learning in contexts ranging from the classroom (see Arnold, Warner, & Osborne, 2006) to the workplace (see Raelin, 2008).

Box 7.5 includes an illustration with descriptions and questions adapted from **Kolb's model of experiential learning**. By targeting each quadrant, you can more effectively describe your learning around the cycle. Box 7.6 suggests an activity to get you started in that process.

## BOX 7.5 Kolb's Model of Experiential Learning

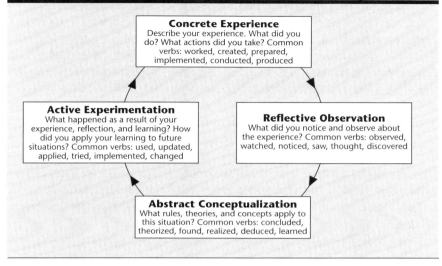

**Concrete Experience**
Describe your experience. What did you do? What actions did you take? Common verbs: worked, created, prepared, implemented, conducted, produced

**Active Experimentation**
What happened as a result of your experience, reflection, and learning? How did you apply your learning to future situations? Common verbs: used, updated, applied, tried, implemented, changed

**Reflective Observation**
What did you notice and observe about the experience? Common verbs: observed, watched, noticed, saw, thought, discovered

**Abstract Conceptualization**
What rules, theories, and concepts apply to this situation? Common verbs: concluded, theorized, found, realized, deduced, learned

# How Can Critical Incidents Demonstrate My Learning?

The final stage of learning in Kolb's model is active experimentation, in which a person takes what he or she has learned and applies it to future events. The concrete experience that led to the learning in the first place is

## BOX 7.6 Using the Kolb Model

Ask a partner to question you about your learning in an area you plan to petition for credit. The questions should target each stage of the cycle.

1. What did you do? (concrete experience)
2. What did you notice? (observations and reflections)
3. What did you conclude as a result of what happened? (abstract conceptualization)
4. How did you apply your learning to future situations? (active experimentation)

Consider having your partner record your responses. This is a good warm-up activity for writing the experiential learning narrative, especially for oral learners.

sometimes called a **critical incident**, and to understand exactly what a critical incident is, we can look to the theories of Stephen Brookfield.

Brookfield is an acclaimed scholar of adult learning, having authored 14 books on the subject and done research and writing on adult teaching, critical thinking, discussion methods, critical theory, and critical pedagogy. He currently holds the title of Distinguished University Professor at the University of St. Thomas in Minneapolis-St. Paul, Minnesota, is the 2008 recipient of CAEL's Morris T. Keeton Award, and was inducted into the International Adult and Continuing Education Hall of Fame in 2009.

According to Brookfield (2006), "usually critical [incidents] are considered as significant by us because they are unexpected, they take us by surprise" (p. 68); a critical incident is also vividly remembered "because it was particularly fulfilling or because it was particularly frustrating. Most probably it is an incident that leaves [a person] somewhat puzzled by its layers and complexities" (p. 46).

Like Kolb, however, Brookfield believes that the greatest impact of a critical incident, the true learning, arises from the process of critical reflection on the event—especially from asking questions that recognize and then disrupt any assumptions about how the event happened and why and how the individual responded. In this way, a critical incident can change ways of thinking, attitudes, or actions. Faced with challenging problems like handling an irate customer, troubleshooting a computer systems crash, coping with an ineffective project manager, keeping a meeting on task, and other such events, adult learners receive valuable insight on what to do differently in the future.

In addition, a detailed description of a critical incident, and your response to it, is a powerful testimony to your learning that can be included in a prior learning portfolio. To help you thoughtfully reflect on a critical incident, take a look at Box 7.7.

## Reflection-in-Action

Besides reflecting on something that has already occurred, some theorists believe that reflection-in-action is also a useful learning tool. Reflection-in-action is very much like thinking on your feet. It involves the ability to think about what you are doing *while* you are doing it. This concept was first introduced by Donald Schöen (1983) in his book *The Reflective Practitioner*, and, like all of the theories discussed in this chapter, remains a capstone in the field of adult learning.

Schöen (1987) states that when faced with complex problems, students and professionals are most successful when they practice this skill of

## BOX 7.7   Reflection on Critical Incidents

Critical incidents, when combined with feedback and reflection, provide learning opportunities. Use these questions to analyze a critical incident:

1. Describe a critical incident and your role in the event. What happened? What did you do? How did you react?
2. At what point during the incident did you feel most engaged with what was happening?
3. At what point during the incident did you feel most distanced from what was happening?
4. What action that anyone took during the incident did you find most affirming and helpful?
5. What action that anyone took during the incident did you find most puzzling or confusing?
6. What about the incident surprised you the most? (This could be something about your own reactions to what went on, something that someone else did, or anything else that occurs to you.)
7. In what way did this incident change you? What did you learn from this incident?
8. Describe how this incident influenced your future decision making or behavior. How did future experiences help you more completely understand this incident?

reflection-in-action. Take a look at Box 7.8 for some questions about your own experiences with reflection-in-action.

# How Can Bloom's Taxonomy Be Used in Critical Thinking and Reflection?

Another important educational model that provides insight into learning and PLA is **Bloom's Taxonomy**. Developed in 1956 by a committee led by Benjamin Bloom, this model divides learning into three domains, or categories: cognitive, affective, and psychomotor. The taxonomy's cognitive domain is of particular interest to the PLA student. This domain is concerned mostly with skills having to do with knowledge and comprehension and with intellectual outcomes. The model breaks the domain down even further into more precise and specific levels, each level building upon the previous level,

## BOX 7.8　Remembering Your Own Reflection-in-Action Experiences

- Can you recall a time when you were in an active state of reflecting on what you were doing *while* you were doing it?
- What kinds of questions did you ask yourself in order to resolve the task?
- How did you test out possibilities?
- Which possibilities worked? Which didn't? Why or why not?
- How did this experience influence your actions in future situations?

with the higher levels involving critical thinking. Box 7.9 lists the six levels of the cognitive domain from Bloom's Taxonomy and gives a brief description of each with possible applications to your PLA process.

## BOX 7.9　Adaptation of Bloom's Taxonomy for PLA Students

| LEVEL | DESCRIPTION | KEY WORDS & REFLECTIONS |
|---|---|---|
| Knowledge | What you can recall and describe, such as facts, terms, and basic concepts. | What, where, when, which, how. Can you describe, define, recall, name, and explain your knowledge? |
| Understanding | Describing, clarifying, and explaining the concepts, facts, or ideas. | Demonstrate, compare, interpret, clarify. Can you explain your knowledge in your own words? |
| Application | Demonstrating how the concepts, facts, or ideas can be used. | Apply, experiment, do. How did you apply your knowledge to a specific situation? |
| Analysis | Examining your decisions and actions in more detail. | Explain, categorize, deduct, problem solve, why. Why did you arrive at your conclusions about the subject matter? |
| Evaluation | Judging the validity of the decision or action taken. | Evaluate, judge, make recommendations. What recommendations do you have as a result of evaluating your learning? |
| Innovation | Creating or changing something based on your previous learning. | Plan, change, create, innovate. What innovation resulted in your learning? |

Most college-level curricula require a level of critical thinking that is built on a foundation of basic knowledge and understanding. When analyzing a particular course, it is useful to estimate where the majority of the outcomes fit. For instance, some lower-level college courses emphasize knowledge and comprehension, while upper-level courses may require a higher level of application, analysis, and evaluation. It follows that, if a prior learning assessment candidate needs to demonstrate learning at the appropriate level, Bloom's Taxonomy can assist the student in using the proper terms. See Box 7.10 for further exploration of how to apply the taxonomy to course outcomes and your prior learning.

## BOX 7.10   Levels of Critical Thinking

Review a course description and, if available, course outcomes or objectives from a course that closely aligns with your learning. Break the course down by percentages concentrating on each stage of the Kolb model. For instance, a business software applications course may draw 40% from the levels of knowledge and understanding and 60% from application. In contrast, a course in management strategies may draw more equally from all the levels, especially if the student applies the knowledge in critical evaluation of his or her work style, indicating high levels of evaluation and innovation.

## REVIEW

- Learning is an active reflective process that draws upon experience.
- Experiential learning, when compared to classroom learning, has both advantages and drawbacks.
- Applying related theoretical concepts and ideas to a practical experience helps students make their learning more complete.
- Tacit knowledge, often retrieved through reflection and analysis, leads to new learning.
- Many learning experiences use a variety of intelligences.
- The Kolb model of experiential learning includes concrete experience, reflection and observation, abstract conceptualization, and active experimentation. When students use the Kolb model to describe their experiential learning, they can target their narratives to each stage of the process.

- Examining and reflecting on critical incidents assists the learning process.
- The higher levels of critical thinking, as demonstrated in Bloom's Taxonomy, are often required for learning at the college level.

## NEXT STEPS

1. Take a look at Box 7.11 to exercise your knowledge of experiential learning.
2. Review several exercises in this chapter, such as the one in Box 7.12, to begin the process of thinking about your own learning.
3. Conduct research on other learning theories and concepts that can further your understanding of your experiential learning. This research will help you expand on the reflective process you've already started for your prior learning assessment..
4. Spend some time every day for one week writing about your learning.

## BOX 7.11   Apply Learning Concepts

Using the learning concepts from this chapter, read the following descriptions and decide whether you think the student's learning was:

a. Complete
b. Somewhat complete
c. Incomplete

### Andrew

1. As a minister who has been called to difficult circumstances like car accidents and the scene of a suicide, Andrew learned about death and dying. Andrew's knowledge of death and dying concepts comes from his understanding of the Bible.
2. Andrew has read extensively on communication theory and has learned communication concepts from college textbooks. He's applied his understanding of the concepts to numerous experiences involved in television, radio, and ministry.

(continued)

## Tim

1. Currently, Tim is employed as a software developer, and he uses UNIX on a daily basis. Some of the commands he uses less frequently, but he knows that if he reviewed the commands, he would learn them quickly.
2. Tim was assigned to lead several large projects and managed them effectively. His understanding of leadership principles is limited to his IT experience.

## Maria

1. Maria learned first aide and CPR (for adults and children) when she applied for her at-home day care licensure. While employed at Head Start, Maria used her first aid skills to assist children.
2. Maria works as a teacher's aide in a Head Start program. She has attended several literacy conferences and workshops and assisted the lead teacher in the classroom; however, she has not designed curricula or lesson plans.

After you have read through each profile and selected a, b, or c, you may wish to return to Chapter 1 and compare your answers as you review the credits received in their profiles.

## BOX 7.12 Thinking about Learning

1. An adult learner with 20 years of experience on the job and a traditional-aged college student are both attending a course on organizational communication.
   a. Can 20 years of experience be equated with 20 years of learning? Why or why not?
   b. What might be some differences in learning styles between the two students?
2. Describe a time when you faced a problem in a work or volunteer setting. What information did you use to analyze the problem? Did you propose a solution?

# ADDITIONAL RESOURCES

"Michael Polanyi and Tacit Learning" @ http://www.infed.org/thinkers/polanyi.htm
 In this article, the conceptual and theory-based foundations of tacit learning are explained by the author, Mark K. Smith (2003).

"Howard Gardner, Multiple Intelligences and Education" @ http://www.infed.org/thinkers/gardner.htm
 This Web page includes a good discussion of the seven intelligences by Mark K. Smith (2008).

"Big Thinkers: Howard Gardner on Multiple Intelligences" @ http://www.youtube.com/watch?v=iYgO8jZTFuQ
 A YouTube video of Howard Gardner discussing how he developed the theory of multiple intelligences.

"Multiple Intelligences Go to School: Educational Implications of the Theory of Multiple Intelligences" @ http://cct2.edc.org/ccthome/reports/tr4.html
 An article by Gardner and Hatch from the March 1990 *CTE Technical Report*, issue no. 4.

"Practical Intelligence" @ http://www.indiana.edu/~intell/practicalintelligence.shtml
 An overview compiled by John Meunier.

"The Human Intelligence: Historical Influences, Current Controversies, Teaching Resources" @ http://www.indiana.edu/~intell/index.shtml

"Mental Processes: Four Styles of Creative Intelligence" @ http://www.associatedcontent.com/article/2779136/mental_processes_four_styles_of_creative.html?cat=72
 Excerpted on AssociatedContent.com from *Creative Intelligence: Discovering the Innovative Potential in Ourselves and Others* by Alan J. Rowe.

Multiple Intelligences Assessment @ http://literacyworks.org/mi/assessment/findyourstrengths.html
 Find your strengths by answering the questionnaire.

"David A. Kolb on Experiential Learning" @ http://www.infed.org/biblio/b-explrn.htm
 This Web page provides a good discussion of the Kolb model by Mark K. Smith (2001).

"The Kolb Learning Cycle" @ http://www.ldu.leeds.ac.uk/ldu/sddu_multimedia/kolb/kolb_flash.htm
 Multimedia tutorial on Kolb's cycle of learning.

"What Is a 'Critical Incident'?" @ http://www.monash.edu.au/lls/llonline/writing/medicine/reflective/2.xml
 From the Language and Learning Online website at Monash University.

"Teaching Critical Reflection" @ http://www.inspiredliving.com/business/reflection.htm
 The importance of critical reflection is discussed in this InspiredLiving.com article by David Stein (2011).

"Bloom's Taxonomy" @ http://www.odu.edu/educ/roverbau/Bloom/blooms_taxonomy.htm
 This site from Richard C. Overbaugh and Lynn Shultz shows both the new and old versions of Bloom's Taxonomy and poses questions about the new taxonomy.

# Portfolio Planning

## CHAPTER 8

*"After spending years raising our children, I was nervous about entering college. Writing the portfolio helped build my writing confidence and gave me a jump-start when I began my more challenging courses."*

—MARIA, AN ADULT LEARNER

## Why Create a Prior Learning Assessment Portfolio?

Previous chapters dealt with the procedures for earning credit for training (transcripts, military, corporate training, certifications) or through test taking (CLEP, DSST, challenge exams). In this chapter, we begin to delve into the process of portfolio development and assessment. Portfolio-assisted assessment was created to help evaluate the types of college-level learning that are not measured by other methods.

## In Preparing the Portfolio, What Type of Assistance Is Available?

Due to the complexity of preparing a portfolio, many colleges offer non-credit workshops or credit-bearing prior learning assessment courses. Assistance may range from a meeting with an advisor to a three-credit course. And of course, this book also contains valuable information and guidance for preparing a PLA portfolio.

## Why Spend Time Planning the Portfolio?

For busy adults, carefully planning the portfolio avoids wasted time and effort. One student recommended reading the entire contents of the portfolio manual or Web site that the college offers, not just scanning them, and keeping a checklist of items that need to be completed. In this way, you'll be sure to meet the deadlines.

# What Are the General Guidelines Evaluators Use for Awarding Credit?

Students should determine the specific criteria the college uses for assessment. Some colleges use the course outcomes or competencies; others use more general standards to determine college-level learning.

The following are general guidelines based on the CAEL standards discussed in Chapter 4. Colleges may set additional criteria.

1. The learning demonstrates college-level achievement.
2. The learning demonstrated is considered at 70% ("C minus" grade) or higher.
3. The learning demonstrates an appropriate level of conceptual or theoretical knowledge as well as application, depending on the subject matter being petitioned.
4. The learning demonstrated is transferable to other contexts.
5. The credits awarded are lined up to fulfill requirements toward a student's degree or goal.
6. The learning for which credit is being petitioned cannot be duplicated by previously earned credit.

## How Is the Portfolio Evaluated?

Generally, the portfolio is evaluated on a pass or no pass basis. In this case, if the portfolio does not pass, the student's grade point average is not affected. A few colleges require evaluators to assign a grade to the portfolio. The evaluator determines the number and type of credits awarded and provides a written explanation for the decision. Box 8.1 describes the options available to evaluators in assigning credit. After assessment, students receive a copy of the credit award along with a written explanation of the evaluator's rationale for the credit decision, and the credit is posted to the student's transcript.

## If the Credit Is Denied, Can I Get My Money Back?

No. The assessment fees, if required by a college or university, are paid up front, regardless of whether credit is awarded or not. Portfolio assessment fees, when required, are like paying tuition for taking a class; tuition is paid no matter what grade is awarded at the end.

## BOX 8.1　Portfolio Assessment Evaluation Options

**Award full credit**
Evaluators can award the full amount of credit petitioned by the student.

**Award partial credit**
Evaluators can award partial credit. Some programs do not allow the evaluator to split credit (e.g., give one credit instead of three).

**Award more credit than requested**
Evaluators may determine that the petition is exceptional and award more credit than the amount a student petitioned.

**Deny credit**
Evaluators can deny credit completely.

**Request an addendum or interview**
Evaluators may request additional information or an interview before making a final credit determination. In such cases, it is advised that the student follow the evaluator's request thoroughly and quickly because a deadline may be imposed. After the addendum material is submitted with the original portfolio or an interview is completed, the evaluator has the option of either awarding or denying the credit.

# What If I Disagree with the Evaluator's Assessment?

Although appeals are generally rare, best practice requires schools to have a policy in place that will allow a student who has been denied credit to request a reassessment of a submitted portfolio. After reviewing an appeal, the evaluator can ask for an addendum, award full or partial credit, or deny the appeal altogether. If an appeal is possible, only one appeal per portfolio can be made. Even if the student is still unhappy with the results after an appeal, a second appeal cannot be made.

# What Steps Will I Take to Prepare and Submit the Portfolio?

Box 8.2 lists the steps in developing and submitting a portfolio, along with a general description of each step and a column where you can track your progress and deadlines.

## BOX 8.2   Portfolio Process

| STEPS | DESCRIPTION | DATE |
|---|---|---|
| 1. Discover | Discover sources of learning. Prepare a preliminary list of the courses that best match the learning and the degree plan. Request letters of verification and begin gathering supporting documentation. | |
| 2. Write | Draft and write prior learning narratives or competency statements. | |
| 3. Organize and edit | Organize supporting documentation and compile portfolio contents. Determine final credit petition. Edit writing. | |
| 4. Submit | Submit portfolio and pay the assessment fee, if required, to appropriate office. | |
| 5. Receive notification | Receive formal notification by letter on credit determination. | |
| 6. Credit recorded | Credit awarded is transcripted by the college's registrar. | |

# How Long Should the Portfolio Be?

The length of the portfolio depends largely on the number of credits being petitioned and the complexity of the subject matter. Students should edit the portfolio and select supporting documentation to avoid redundancy. A well prepared portfolio, including forms, narratives, and supporting documentation, may be 15 pages or longer.

If a student is petitioning different schools, divisions, or departments, (i.e., requesting credit in courses from the School of Business and courses from the College of Arts and Sciences), it will speed up the evaluation process to prepare a number of smaller portfolios. This way, instead of submitting one large portfolio to one department, then passing it on to another, etc., each faculty member is able to assess independently.

# How Long Will It Take Me to Create a Portfolio?

The amount of time it takes to complete a portfolio varies greatly: it can take anywhere from several weeks to several months, depending on work/family commitments, the ability to locate and secure supporting documentation, the amount of credit being petitioned, and school or course requirements. Perhaps the biggest factor in determining how long it will take to complete a portfolio is the amount of credit being petitioned. A portfolio that is targeting between 9 and 15 credits may take four or more months to compile.

If you take a PLA portfolio course, your course may require that you have a completed portfolio by the end of the course. The length of these courses can vary from five weeks to a full semester. Other courses or programs may give you time beyond the course itself to finish your portfolio; this can range from six months to two years or perhaps even the length of your program.

Also note that some colleges allow students to submit multiple portfolios over a period of time, while others have one submission deadline. At this point, it once again becomes clear that you must take charge of your PLA process and know exactly what your program's specific policies are.

One more very important note about time considerations for the portfolio process: many students think that they can submit a portfolio up to their graduation date, which is an incorrect assumption that often causes a great amount of frustration for the students, their advisors, and the college registrars. **You must allow time for the assessment of the portfolio and for the transcription of the credit before graduation.** It may take several weeks for the portfolio to be assessed and recorded on your transcript. Remember this fact and manage your time effectively, especially as you get closer to graduation.

## How Do I Select the Course or Outcomes and Number of Credits to Petition?

Determining the courses or outcomes to petition is a process of discovery that is refined throughout the entire portfolio process. Ultimately, the evaluator determines the final credit award, but the student targets the areas he or she thinks the evaluator will use to determine credit.

Some students overestimate the amount of credit they could realistically receive; others underestimate the amount. One student stated, "The best advice I have is to work closely with an advisor. Initially, I thought I'd petition for six elective credits based on my paralegal work, but my advisor encouraged me to petition for nine credits based on three legal courses. I was glad I followed her advice."

Box 8.3 provides some guidance on figuring out what courses or outcomes to petition for, but it is always a good idea to seek support from an academic advisor.

## BOX 8.3    Process of Selecting Credits to Petition

1. Consult your learning inventory created using Appendix 2.
2. Compare your learning to the outcomes for a college course by consulting course descriptions and outcomes (see Chapter 9). Eliminate sources of learning that would not be considered college level. For instance, one student planned a large wedding for over a year; however, even though she learned about negotiating, planning, and budgeting during her wedding preparation, she could not match the experience closely to the outcomes of a college course.
3. Refine your list of course petitions against your goals with the assistance of an advisor. Check for duplication of previously earned credit (see also Chapter 3 on PLA planning).
4. Revise the list, as needed, when you prepare your portfolio. Thinking about your prior learning during the portfolio process may help you uncover areas of learning that you did not previously consider.

# What If My Learning Doesn't Fit Very Neatly into a Category?

Students whose learning doesn't fit neatly into a college course or competency will benefit from taking a prior learning assessment course or talking with a faculty member or advisor.

One student, who was interested in petitioning for credit after completing two tours in Vietnam, was advised to submit his entire body of work for assessment. After some revisions, the student was awarded 30 credits in a variety of subject areas, including global issues, photojournalism, radio broadcasting, screenwriting, and adult spiritual life and growth.

Another student's learning came from his 10 years as a recovering alcoholic. His commitment to Alcoholics Anonymous led him to open several AA chapters in local prisons. His learning didn't fit neatly into a category, but the college he attended awarded competency credits in areas such as motivation and leadership and alcohol addiction. Some colleges provide databases or lists of possible courses or competencies that can be used to petition for credit.

# Can I Earn Credit for Travel Experiences and Significant Family Events?

One of the most challenging steps for students in the PLA process involves identifying their prior learning as related to a college course's objectives. It is possible to earn credit for travel or family experience, but as always, college-level learning must be evident. Just because you have experience does not mean you have college-level learning—CAEL's first PLA standard (Chapter 4). Also, one of the reasons travel and family experiences can be more difficult to petition for credit is that the learning often does not transfer to broader contexts (see standards 2 and 3 in Chapter 4).

To successfully petition credit for family experience, a student might decide to use a Marriage and Family course from a sociological perspective as a basis for his or her petition. The student's narrative would demonstrate personal learning about marriage and family as well as how the personal experience fits within the broader context of society. The broader context might include an awareness of topics such as dating, intimacy, intercultural communication, relationships, aging, and emerging forms of family as they relate to issues in society. Students who have experience in more than one context—e.g., have taught a premarital counseling course or worked in a nonprofit agency that broadened their awareness of family issues—may have more in-depth learning that would be considered applicable in a number of settings.

A student who has traveled extensively might focus on Intercultural Communication, Art History, or Managing Diverse Teams. Again, whatever the experience, it must be tied to an academic discipline and show a depth of knowledge that would be considered college level. A general recollection of highlights or the submission of travel logs alone may not yield the depth of learning required. However, a military/work experience, immersion in another culture, extensive study abroad, or in-depth cross-cultural training may be the basis for learning that is the equivalent of a college-level course. If your travel experience does not qualify for assessment per se but you have acquired language through your travels, you might consider taking a CLEP language exam.

The bottom line is that, as with all PLA, your travel and family learning must be congruent with an academic discipline and the college-level learning of that discipline. Both depth and breadth are necessary in order for learning to be college level.

# What Are Some of the Typical Contents of the Prior Learning Assessment Portfolio?

Depending on the college, contents of the portfolio may include some, or all, of the components listed in Box 8.4.

## BOX 8.4 Typical Portfolio Contents

| CONTENTS | DESCRIPTION |
| --- | --- |
| Title page | Title, name, identification number, contact information, and date. |
| Table of contents | Lists the contents of the portfolio in order. |
| Goal statements or forms with a signature of authenticity | 1. Statement of student's educational goals.<br>2. Statement on how prior learning assessment relates to educational goals.<br>3. Statement on courses or outcomes being petitioned for credit.<br>4. Statement of authenticity and signature.<br>Note: Some colleges have students notarize the statement of authenticity. |
| Learning chronology | Résumé, learning chart, or learning autobiography with experience in chronological order. |
| Prior learning narrative or competency statements (repeated for each subject or outcome being petitioned) | Extensive learning narrative or competency statements matching the student's learning to the college-level course or outcomes being petitioned. |
| Index of supporting documentation | List of supporting documentation that verifies the learning. |
| Supporting documentation | Supporting documentation, numbered with captions. |

(continued)

| Transcript copies and degree plan | Working copies of degree plan and transcripts to verify that credit being petitioned meets requirements for the student's goals and is not duplicated by previously earned credit. |
| --- | --- |
| Evaluation forms | Form used by evaluator to write the credit recommendation. |

## What Is a Learning Chronology, and Why Include One in the Portfolio?

Preparing the learning chronology helps the learner recall and organize their learning experiences. As students prepare this part of the portfolio, they begin to reflect on their learning.

The completed learning chronology helps the evaluator understand the context in which a student's learning took place. Depending on the college's requirements, students may include one of the following options in their portfolios:

- Résumé or expanded résumé with or without training records;
- Learning chart that demonstrates what a student knows and can do;
- Learning autobiography or life history paper;
- Chronological record

A learning chronology provides students with an appreciation of the knowledge they gained in a number of settings and the ability to see the threads in their learning.

## If I Include a Résumé in My Portfolio, What Format Should I Use?

Many students include a standard résumé in their portfolios as either part or all of their learning chronology. As mentioned earlier, colleges differ in what they require a student to submit for the learning chronology section of a portfolio, and a résumé is often an option. The résumé included in your portfolio can be easily tailored to the prior learning portfolio by including the knowledge, skills, competencies, and training gained in areas being petitioned for credit. Or, if you have had relevant learning in a volunteer capacity, the experience can be added to a chronological or skills résumé.

# What Are Some Warm-Up Activities Used to Prepare a Learning Chronology?

In Chapter 1, you created a learning inventory using Appendix 2. Your inventory, which includes the skills and competencies you researched on O*Net.com, is a great resource for creating your learning chronology.

Another exercise you can do is to reflect on the various roles you play. Adult students juggle many roles and responsibilities in their personal and professional lives. Box 8.5 guides you through a reflection on your own list of duties and roles.

## BOX 8.5 Determining Roles and Responsibilities

1. Write 8 to 10 different roles or responsibilities you currently juggle or have juggled in the past. These roles may help you identify areas of significant learning. Here's an example:
   - Parent
   - Student
   - Spouse
   - Son
   - Front-line supervisor
   - Union negotiator
   - Home-budget manager
   - Volunteer for Boy Scouts
2. Once you've created your list, take some time to answer these questions to reflect on your roles.
   - What roles do you juggle every day?
   - What roles often collide or are in conflict?
   - What roles provide the most satisfaction?
   - What competencies do you demonstrate when you are in each role (see Appendix 2, Part 3 for competency verbs)?

Drawing and labeling a timeline is another excellent prewriting activity. A timeline will help you recall significant life events in chronological order. See Box 8.6 for some tips on creating your own timeline.

## BOX 8.6 Timeline

1. Draw a line horizontally across your page using paper or computer software. Starting with your high school graduation date, cross mark the line in increments of five years. You might even project five years into the future to indicate goals.
2. Plot significant events by the year on your timeline. You could include personal experiences, work, military service, and volunteer experiences.
3. Draw branches off the significant events and add key words describing the skills and knowledge you acquired during each time period.
4. Reflect on your timeline events by answering these questions:
5. What were the major turning points in your life? (e.g., the birth of your first child, your first job or promotion)
6. What did you learn? What skills did you acquire?
7. What events were dissatisfying at the time but proved to be valuable learning experiences? (e.g., a divorce, a change in jobs)
8. What did you learn? How did it affect your future goals?

# What Does a Learning Chart Include?

Another format often used to present a learning chronology is a learning chart. As with all learning chronology formats, the purpose of the learning chart is to help you explore your learning—the knowledge and abilities you've gained from experience. A learning chart can be formatted as a table and placed horizontally on a page like the excerpt shown in Box 8.7.

## BOX 8.7   Learning Chart

| SOURCE OF LEARNING | EXPERIENCE | COMPETENCIES (AS RELATED TO COURSE PETITIONS) |
|---|---|---|
| Places and Dates | Primary Responsibilities | Knowledge and Abilities |
| • Radio Station KCRS Public Relations 2008–2010 | • Assist radio station in public relations and community building efforts. | • Assist in preparation of public relations materials. <br> • Write, edit, and proofread public relations materials. |

(continued)

| SOURCE OF LEARNING | EXPERIENCE | COMPETENCIES (AS RELATED TO COURSE PETITIONS) |
|---|---|---|
| | | • Measure, reevaluate, and report efforts.<br>• Write fact sheets, news releases, and grants.<br>• Set up and implement publicity efforts such as trade shows, fairs, and fundraisers.<br>• Develop and maintain contacts with advertisers and community leaders.<br>• Utilize word processing software. |

Continue chart with each major source of learning.

# What Is a Learning Autobiography?

A learning autobiography is yet another way to present your learning chronology. It is like a résumé in essay form, but may take the information found in a traditional résumé a bit further by including more personal information. In this way, the learning autobiography serves as an even more complete introduction to a student and offers insight into any gaps in the work history, such as when a student took time off to raise a child or start a business.

A learning autobiography differs from a learning narrative (discussed later in this chapter) in that it covers the full range of your experience after high school. Boxes 8.8 and 8.9 include questions and opportunities for reflection to help you prepare a learning autobiography.

## BOX 8.8 Questions for Learning Autobiography

- Where did you learn what you know, what was your title, and what years did you serve in this position?
- Where and when did you decide to pursue your current goal?
- Who influenced you?
- Why was this experience significant?
- What did you learn at each stage that you didn't know before?
- How did the experiences you had change your beliefs?

(continued)

- What deeply held values have come from your cultural and gender experiences?
- What messages did you receive (or not receive) about the importance of a college education?
- What are some central ideas or philosophies that you have developed in regard to your field?
- If someone were to watch you perform, what knowledge, skills, and abilities would they witness? What personal qualities would they observe?
- What level of learning have you achieved?

## BOX 8.9   Life Changes

Writing an autobiography is an opportunity to think about the changes you've experienced.

For example:

- Changes in relationships and families
- Changes in the workplace
- Changes in your community
- Changes in your beliefs

As you write, tune in to the **metacognitive process**: the process of knowing that occurs when monitoring one's own awareness and judgment. Perhaps you can recall **transformational learning** experiences: life-altering insights that made you perceive yourself and the world differently. Your expanded sense of meaning may occur gradually or suddenly. In transformational learning, even more important than what we know is how we know.

# How Can I Organize My Learning Autobiography?

Like most basic essays, your learning autobiography should have an introduction, a body, and a conclusion. Your introduction should be brief, with the bulk of the information in the body of the document. In the body, make sure to discuss the context of your learning, any specific training received, and what you learned. Then provide a brief summary of how your learning fits in with your educational goals. The excerpts in Box 8.10 are from actual adult students' portfolios.

# Box 8.10 Learning Autobiography Excerpts

**Introduction:**
**State learning from early years succinctly and move quickly to learning after high school.**

"My family moved from a small town in New Jersey, where I attended elementary school, to Southern California, which at the time seemed like moving to a foreign country. I grew up thinking that I'd follow in my father's and grandfather's footsteps and take over the family construction business. However, when the construction business took a downward turn, I entered the world of computers. Little did I know that I'd spend the majority of my adult life in the IT field."

**Body:**
**Include specifics on the context of the learning (when and where) and what was learned (knowledge, skills, and abilities)**

"In 2010, I was transferred to the newly formed customer support department and became a customer representative. My responsibilities included responding to all complaint calls and troubleshooting problems related to the rollout of our services. At the same time I was learning UNIX and started to converse with the software engineers."

**Specify the types of training received.**

"In 2007 when I started a day care, I completed CPR, first aid, and advanced CPR training through the American Montessori Society."
"After raising my children, I found that working as an early childhood educator was fulfilling because of the numerous training opportunities I received through the Head Start program. I also attended a conference on teaching in a multicultural classroom, which consisted of sessions on such topics as diversity, learning styles, and teaching manipulatives (mathematics)."

**Conclusion:**
**Summarize the learning and state educational and career goals.**

"I made a promise to myself that I would complete a bachelor's degree before my sons finished college."

# What Types of Transitional Phrases Are Useful for Writing the Learning Autobiography?

To help the reader follow the chronology of events, you can use transitional words and phrases like those presented in Box 8.11.

## BOX 8.11 Examples of Transitional Phrases

**Chronological:**
- During 2000–2004, I worked for . . .
- Summarizing the next five years . . .
- In 2009, the business . . .
- By 2010, I was . . .
- In May of 2011, I took one of the biggest risks of my life . . .
- For the next 20 years, I held numerous positions in the telecommunication industry.

**Topical:**
- My skill set had grown tremendously, so I was ready for a new challenge.
- Even though my personal life took a downward turn, my spiritual life and volunteer activities during this time were gratifying.
- During the next six years, I received training from the police department in a number of areas, including . . .
- After experiencing a second downsizing in the organization where I worked, I looked more closely at my goals.
- During the next five years, I made up for my string of poor financial decisions.
- In the aftermath of Hurricane Katrina, my family and I relocated.

# What Is a Prior Learning Narrative and How Is It Different Than a College Research Paper?

The learning narrative differs from the learning autobiography in that it is not a complete chronology of your lifelong learning: instead, it is a more detailed discussion of your learning specific to the course or subject matter you are petitioning. In other words, you will need to write a learning narrative for each course being petitioned. The narrative is not a term paper or research paper, although definitions or theories from books may be woven into it. The narrative is written in first person, using "I" (e.g., I concluded, I revised). The writer uses specific stories, examples, and details to describe learning related to the subject matter. The prior learning narrative may also be known as

- A prior learning essay
- An experiential learning essay
- A portfolio narrative
- Competency statements
- A learning narrative

The questions in Boxes 8.8 and 8.9 for the autobiography are also very relevant for writing a narrative, but for the narrative you will want to give more in-depth and personal insights into your learning, especially as it pertains to the specific course and outcomes. The rest of this book will give you ideas on how to write a successful learning narrative, and Appendix 7 includes an excerpt for you to see what one might look like.

## What Are Competency Statements?

Competency statements are sentences that identify what you know, what you can do (skills and abilities), and your level of achievement. In programs such as education or health care, competency statements may be used in lieu of the prior learning narrative. An example of a competency statement might be "I know and can use the principles of classroom techniques, both verbal and nonverbal, to encourage students to stay on task." See Appendix 8 for more examples of how competency statements can be worded and formatted.

## What Are Some Guidelines for Adapting Your Learning Autobiography to the Audience—the Evaluator?

Another key to effective essay writing is to adapt your writing to the audience; whoever is going to be reading your essay. In this case, your audience is the evaluator. Below are keys to streamlining your learning autobiography for your portfolio assessor.

1. The evaluator is particularly interested in understanding the context for learning that a student will petition.

2. The evaluator can award credit only for learning after high school, so the emphasis should be placed on learning after high school.
3. Evaluators are busy college instructors who appreciate succinct writing, so students should stick to the page limit requirements.
4. The learning autobiography does not need to reveal highly personal, sensitive information that is not relevant to the subject areas being petitioned.

## REVIEW

- Colleges use the portfolio method to assess the types of college-level learning that are not measured by other assessment methods.
- Spending time planning the portfolio saves students time and energy.
- Evaluators can award full or partial credit, deny credit, or request an addendum.
- Selecting the course or outcomes and number of credits for which to petition is a process of discovery that can be refined while preparing the portfolio with the assistance of an advisor.
- Students should follow the college's requirements for writing a learning chronology, learning autobiography, or résumé.
- Preparing a learning chronology helps students recognize threads and patterns in their lives and appreciate the learning that has resulted from experience.

## NEXT STEPS

1. Review the portfolio assessment procedures at your college.
2. Review the steps for completing your portfolio and create a checklist and timeline for completion.
3. Reflect on your life's events by completing a warm-up activity such as a timeline.
4. Use the learning chronology to refine your selection of areas to petition.
5. Receive feedback on your draft from an online writing lab (see Additional Resources) or an editor.

## ADDITIONAL RESOURCES

Purdue University's online writing lab (OWL) @ http://owl.english.purdue.edu Excellent resource for college-level writing.

Annotated Bibliography for PLAR @ http://fcis.oise.utoronto.ca/~plar/database/
intro.html
University of Toronto's database of publications on Prior Learning Assessment and
Recognition (PLAR)
Michelson, E., Mandell, A., & Contributors. (2004). *Portfolio development and the
assessment of prior learning: perspectives, models, and practices*. Sterling, VA:
Stylus Publishing.

# Research, Organization, and Writing Strategies

## CHAPTER 9

## Why Is It Critical to Get Clarification from the College on the Format?

Although there are similarities, every college has different requirements for the format, style, and length of the written portion of the portfolio. You should request clarification, or better yet, view sample student portfolios that have been evaluated, instead of submitting a portfolio that misses the mark. Also note that some colleges prefer a formal written narrative while others prefer competency statements or charts to demonstrate learning.

## Why Research and Organize My Thoughts First?

Students have described writing the portfolio narrative or competency statements as a challenging but rewarding task, and as this book has stated before, research will save you time and energy. It is not a good idea to sit down and start writing a diary of random thoughts and stories related to your learning. Research helps you stay on track by targeting the course topics, key words, key theories, concepts, or skills to be covered. Also, conducting research helps determine and describe your level of achievement.

## What Course Research Is Useful to Conduct?

Since colleges frequently revise courses and outcomes, you should seek the most up-to-date information available. Box 9.1 offers examples of what kinds of course information PLA students need and possible resources for finding them.

# BOX 9.1   Course Research

| TYPE OF RESEARCH | AVAILABILITY | USEFULNESS TO PLA STUDENT |
|---|---|---|
| Course Description<br>• States number of credits (semester or quarter hours).<br>• Course number indicates lower or upper level.<br>• Describes course. | Readily available from<br>• College Web site<br>• Published bulletin | Somewhat useful.<br>• Good starting point.<br>• Determines college level.<br>• Determines credit award (semester or quarter).<br>• Description may list key subject areas. |
| Course Outcomes<br>• Sentences that describe the learning results.<br>• Provides topic areas. | Somewhat available from<br>• Course syllabus<br>• College Web site<br>• Academic department<br>• Textbooks at the beginning of each chapter: "After reading this chapter, you will be able to…" | Very useful.<br>• Helps students understand the expectations for passing the course. |
| Course Syllabus<br>• Instructor-specific summary of topics and requirements. | Less readily available from<br>• Instructor<br>• Academic department | Somewhat useful.<br>• May identify key content areas (see next question/ section about syllabi). |
| Course Textbook(s)<br>• Books required or recommended for the course. | Readily available from<br>• College bookstore<br>• Perhaps online<br>• College library<br>• Maybe through a digital book resource like Books24X7 (ask your library) | Somewhat useful.<br>• Describes key theoretical principles or concepts.<br>• Helps student understand the depth and breadth of learning required.<br>• Highlights key terms and vocabulary associated with college-level subjects. |
| Subject-Matter-Related Materials<br>• Books<br>• Web sites<br>• Academic articles | Readily available but<br>• Quality varies.<br>• Student should select highly academic, credible, and relevant sources. | Somewhat useful.<br>• May help remind students of key theoretical principles or concepts related to the subject matter. |
| Interview with Evaluator | May or may not be available.<br>• May be available up front to discuss general guidelines for the portfolio.<br>• Generally unavailable for feedback during the writing process due to need for objectivity in the evaluation process. (Students may obtain feedback on writing from a portfolio course instructor or advisor.) | Useful.<br>• Evaluator has expertise in subject matter and level of learning.<br>• Evaluator may indicate preferences, such as types of supporting documentation to include in the portfolio. |

# What Elements of a Course Syllabus Are Useful for Writing about My Prior Learning?

A course **syllabus** may provide some guidelines for students who want to petition for learning based on the course. Not all course syllabi have the same elements. If you are able to find a very detailed syllabus, as illustrated in Box 9.2, you will have a firm grip on the course requirements and, more importantly, the course outcomes.

## BOX 9.2   Syllabus Research

| ELEMENTS OF SYLLABUS | PRIOR LEARNING ASSESSMENT |
|---|---|
| Course description | Identifies number of credits and level of course (lower level, upper level). The most useful course descriptions provide specific topic areas. |
| Course objectives or outcomes | Clear descriptions of the learning gained as a result of taking the course. May indicate key principles or concepts covered. |
| Explanations of assignments | Identifies key areas, principles, or skills covered. |
| Course breakdown or breakdown of assignments | May pinpoint subject areas that are emphasized. |
| Requirements for the final exam or project | May help determine the level of achievement required. |

# What Is the Difference between Lower-Division (or Lower-Level) and Upper-Division (or Upper-Level) Coursework?

At most colleges, lower-division classes are numbered 100–299. Lower-division courses may be introductory, foundational, or survey courses. Upper-level courses, usually numbered 300–499, are more advanced courses that may have prerequisites (courses that must be completed first). Community colleges do not offer upper-division classes for the simple reason that they do not offer four-year degree programs. Students usually take lower-division courses before enrolling in upper-division courses.

Some colleges' departments will base the course level on "time period covered." For example, a 100-level American History I course might be a general overview spanning over 200 years—1620 to 1865—for example. A

300-level course, however, might detail a shorter span of years, covering finer points relevant to the topic—The Vietnam War 1955 to 1980.

Also note that courses are divided into undergraduate and graduate levels. Undergraduate-level coursework is usually taken to complete your first degree after high school: either an associate degree or a bachelor's degree. Graduate-level coursework is offered to students who are working on their master's or doctorate degrees.

In the case of petitioning for prior learning credit, some colleges require that prerequisite or lower-division courses be fulfilled (through coursework or by portfolio) before a student petitions for upper-division credits. Additionally, the student should be aware that upper-division courses may require an advanced level of learning.

## Can I Match My Learning with Course Descriptions from Other Accredited Colleges?

This will depend on the college's prior learning assessment policies. Some colleges allow students to petition for courses from accredited colleges other than the one they are attending if the college the student is attending does not offer the course.

For instance, if a student has extensive background in intercultural communication, and the college does not offer a corresponding course, the student may be allowed to find a course description from another accredited college to use as a basis for awarding credit (see Box 9.3). In this case, the credit would be awarded at the institution where the student was enrolled and transcripted under a general category, such as "communication, lower-division elective."

## What If There Are Outcomes in the Course That I Don't Know?

Students who petition for full credit in a course—usually three credits—should be able to demonstrate their learning in the majority of the course outcomes. A careful review of a recent textbook can help you discover any possible deficiencies. Sometimes studying a minor component will bring your knowledge up to par. If you do not have learning in a significant area covered in the course, it is best to select another course to petition. Some institutions offer theory workshops to help students master this missing component of their learning.

## BOX 9.3   Locating Accredited Colleges' Course Descriptions

Here are some ideas for searching the Internet for another accredited college's course listings and descriptions.

1. A search engine is always a good place to start.
   - Enter your search criteria. For example, an "intercultural communication" course description may be found by entering "intercultural communication" + "course description" in the search box.
   - Scroll through the results and select sites with ".edu" in the Web address, indicating courses offered in educational institutions (avoid ".org" and ".com" sites).
2. There are also certain Web sites designed to help you locate colleges that offer a specific major, subject area, and even course descriptions (e.g., http://www.petersons.com, http://collegessearch. collegeboard.com, or http://www.courseatlas.com).
3. If you already know the college you want to look at, go to their Web site.
   - Search through the college Web site's academic departments and lists of majors (e.g., Intercultural Studies or Communications) to find course titles that sound appropriate.
   - Once you've found course titles, see if you can locate a course description, usually found in online course catalogs or bulletins.
   - If you can't find one on the Web site, you can always contact the academic department for a description.
   - Print the description, URL, publication date, and name of the college for future reference.

# Can I Adapt Course Outcomes to Reflect Experiential Learning?

Some colleges allow students to adapt course outcomes to better reflect the criteria for experiential learning. Box 9.4 shows an example, provided by Donna Younger, of how one student rewrote an outcome for a course in business communication.

The outcome on the syllabus for the course included a reference to a specific text that students were required to read. The fundamental knowledge gained from reading this text is described in the original outcome as being related to elements of negotiation and negotiation skills. In the rewrite of the outcome, because the student's knowledge comes from experience and not from the specific text, her knowledge may differ slightly in the specifics, but the "fundamental" elements remain. Also note how the new outcome not only covers a discussion of negotiation principles, but also includes applying those principles to a real life experience.

## BOX 9.4    Revising Outcomes

| OUTCOME FROM BUSINESS COMMUNICATION SYLLABUS | REVISED OUTCOME |
| --- | --- |
| "Students will be able to articulate the four steps in negotiation from Simpson's *The Art of Negotiation* and describe how they might be used." | "Students will identify one model of negotiation, describe the negotiation process, and use it to critique a case study drawn from their work experience." |

# If I'm Required to Write a Narrative, What Is the Standard Organization and Format?

Just like an essay, the standard structure for the narrative includes an introduction, body, and conclusion. Box 9.5 gives you more details on what to include in each portion for your narrative. You can also refer back to Chapter 8's discussion of organizing a learning autobiography.

## BOX 9.5 Standard Narrative Format

**Introduction**
Introduces the topic, provides a unifying thesis, and introduces the structure of the narrative. Main points covered in the narrative may be listed.

**Body**
Topics are divided topically or chronologically (see the discussion on organizing the main points of your narrative that follows). The body develops each topic further, providing supporting information and ideas. Some colleges require boldfaced headings.

**Conclusion**
Restates your thesis and the most meaningful points of the narrative and includes your closing ideas.

# How Do I Use a Prewriting Technique Such as a Mind Map?

You've already explored several prewriting exercises with your learning inventory, your roles and responsibilities list, and your timeline. All of these exercises help you put thoughts on the page and avoid writer's block. Another prewriting exercise that can really help you brainstorm ideas is a mind map. Mind maps are diagrams that help you recall and visualize the structure of related details. You can hand draw a mind map, use a graphics program, or use the drawing toolbar in a word processing program. There are also free concept- and mind-mapping software tools on the Internet that can help you create really dynamic diagrams (see Additional Resources).

The basic idea is to start at the center of the page and write the name of the course in the middle. Then draw spokes that correspond to outcomes or topic areas. Next, draw small branches off the spokes and add related key words or descriptions. You can even try inserting a SmartArt graphic using a Microsoft program, such as Word or PowerPoint. This should be a brainstorming process, so let the ideas come quickly. Later you can use your mind map to develop a formal outline.

# What Are Some Ways to Organize the Main Points of My Narrative?

Box 9.6 explains a few organizational strategies commonly used for learning narratives. However, you should use the organizational structure recommended by your college. No matter which format you use, make sure to address all of the major outcomes you identified in your course research. You may need to combine some topics in order to maintain clarity and conciseness.

# What Are Some General and Specific Editing Tips?

In the final step of writing the narrative, you should thoroughly edit the contents because evaluators place high expectations on quality content when making credit determinations. You are strongly encouraged to use writing resources offered by the college, such as an OWL (online writing lab). Purdue University has an excellent OWL (http://owl.english.purdue.edu/) that provides all kinds of information about basic writing principles as well as more specific information about styles for citations and bibliog-

## BOX 9.6   Learning Narrative Organization

**By Course Description**
For the course Business Writing

Here is the course description as published in the 2010 bulletin:
BA202 Business Writing (3 credits)
This course addresses business communications, including letters, memos, reports, proposals, and presentations.

*Structure:* This narrative will demonstrate my writing competencies (knowledge and skills) gained from preparing:
- Letters
- Memos
- Reports
- Proposals
- Presentations

**By Key Topics**
For the course Management of Human Resources

*Structure:* This narrative will demonstrate my learning related to the following human resources areas:
- Interviewing
- Employment offer
- Customer service
- Compensation and motivation
- Health care and mental health benefits
- Relevant OSHA laws
- ADA policies
- Training
- Ethical considerations

**By Course Outcomes**
For the course Public Speaking

*Structure:* The following discussion of my learning will follow each of the course outcomes, which include:
- Demonstrating the ability to recognize and select appropriate topics for oral presentations.
- Demonstrating the ability to logically organize and provide oral presentations.

(continued)

- Demonstrating the ability to locate and cite sources of information.
- Demonstrating the ability to use effective vocal delivery techniques.
- Demonstrating the ability to adapt speeches to specific audiences.
- Demonstrating the ability to utilize technology to compile information and enhance oral communication.
- Evaluating speeches using listening, reasoning, and content analysis skills.
- Incorporating critical thinking skills and argumentation principles into speech analysis and presentations.

### By Chronology
For the course Web Page Design

*Structure:* My experience related to designing Web pages is best described by using the following building blocks:
- Understanding the client-server system and the Internet.
- Using HTML to create graphs and charts and to format pages.
- Using Web-authoring software to create animation and effects.
- Refining Web pages to be user friendly.
- Creating a company intranet.

---

raphies. Or you might ask a classmate, friend, or colleague for editing assistance.

## General Editing Tips

1. Check that the content and illustrations match the course.
2. Check for sufficient details to demonstrate learning.
3. Check for accuracy.
4. Check for grammatical and spelling errors.
5. Check the flow so that the illustrations easily unfold for the reader.

## Specific Editing Tips

1. Don't rely on the spelling and grammar checker.

   Example: *principal* and *principle* are often used incorrectly.

   Grammar checks may not catch the incorrect use of apostrophes.

   Example: The manager's (possessive when you mean plural) or it's (meaning "it is," when you mean possessive).

2. Avoid clichés or overused phrases.

   Examples:
   - It went without saying
   - Hit the nail on the head
   - My other half
   - Stuck out like a sore thumb
   - I was not the least bit concerned

3. Replace multiple words with one or two.

   Examples:
   In the near future (replace with "Soon")
   With the exception of (replace with "Except for")

4. Watch over-capitalization.

   Capitalize proper names of people, places, organizations, institutions, and corporations.

   Examples:
   I served with John Brown in a volunteer capacity in Colorado.
   I was a customer service representative for SBC Communications, Inc.
   After high school, I transferred to Metro State College of Denver.

5. Check verb and pronoun consistency.

   a. Keep verb tense consistent.

      This can be difficult when shifting from an explanation of a past event to a present revelation. Most commonly, the narrative is written in past tense to reflect prior learning.

   b. Keep pronoun use consistent.

      Use first person (I/we) or second (you), but do not combine the two.

6. Use strong verbs.

   Example: I had an interview with a client. Replace "had" with "conducted."

7. Include the "actor" (subject) with the action verb.

   Before: I remember one instance when adjustments to the project's lifecycle weren't communicated to the stakeholders. (No actor stated)

   After: I remember one instance when I made adjustments to the project's lifecycle, but I failed to communicate the changes to the stakeholders. The results were disastrous.

# What Is Plagiarism and What Steps Can I Take to Avoid It?

Plagiarism is using someone else's written material or work as one's own. Colleges have adopted strict academic honesty policies partly in response to students who are able to easily cut and paste material from the Internet. In addition, many colleges subscribe to services such as www.turnitin.com to detect plagiarism in students' papers. To avoid plagiarism, students should locate a reference manual and use the style of documentation recommended (e.g., APA, MLA) and always use their own original ideas. The general rule is, if in doubt, cite the work. Of course, some knowledge is "common knowledge." You wouldn't need to cite the source for the following statement: President John F. Kennedy was assassinated in Dallas on November 22, 1963.

## Adult Learner Profile

Maria divided her Introduction to Communication narrative into three sections—public speaking, interpersonal communication, and group communication—using the topical approach of organization (see sample in Appendix 7).

## REVIEW

- Make sure that your portfolio builds the right contents and that the content matches your educational plan, your learning, and the course objectives or outcomes.
- Conducting research on the requirements and criteria for evaluation helps maintain focus.
- Using prewriting and editing strategies assists in the writing process.

## NEXT STEPS

1. Search for course descriptions or outcomes closely related to your learning.
2. Conduct research on the requirements for the learning narrative and the topic areas that you will address in the narrative.

3. Try a prewriting strategy such as a mind map to prepare the structure of the narrative and to brainstorm ideas.

4. Write an outline for the narrative based on the mind map or other brainstorming exercise.

## ADDITIONAL RESOURCES

bubbl.us @ http://bubbl.us
> A free online mind mapping tool. No need to download anything, just sign in by creating a username and password.

MindMeister @ http://www.mindmeister.com
> Another online mind mapping tool that offers a free account for 30 days.

The Purdue OWL (Online Writing Lab) @ http://owl.english.purdue.edu
> This Web site offers over 200 free resources on writing, research, grammar, and style.

# Writing about Learning

## CHAPTER 10

After targeting, researching, and organizing the content of your narrative, your next aim is to write the best possible explanation of your learning. In fact, the demonstration of the learning is the most critical ingredient in the portfolio. Some colleges require students to write competency statements that describe learning outcomes; others require a lengthy formal narrative. Either way, the challenge for you is to provide sufficient detail about your learning for the evaluator to make a credit decision. The task requires a description of what was learned about the subject matter with sufficient analysis to demonstrate college-level thinking.

In order to stimulate your recall of past events, consider talking with colleagues about your experiences. To stimulate analysis of key concepts covered in the targeted course, review textbooks or read current literature in the field. Due to the unique experiences and wisdom of each student, no two learning descriptions are alike; in this way, writing the learning narrative is more art than science.

Avoid exaggerating your abilities or roles in projects; on the other hand, don't underplay the scope of your experience and learning. The evaluator is an expert in the field who will recognize if a student fabricates theories or manufactures evidence.

Even though the task is challenging, especially when writing within the confines of course outcomes, the results are rewarding. The road to learning is rarely linear. It is paved with unfortunate incidents and important insights, boredom and breakthroughs, mistakes and momentous events. The opportunity to capture and reflect on prior learning experiences yields new learning.

This chapter presents seven writing strategies for describing experiential learning:

1. Write a detailed description that matches a learning outcome and incorporate key terms.
2. Describe and reflect on a critical incident.
3. Write the steps taken when learning a skill or ability.
4. Integrate definitions and concepts to demonstrate higher levels of learning.
5. Demonstrate problem-solving ability.
6. Write competency statements with strong action verbs.
7. Indicate the level of learning achieved.

There are certainly more writing strategies than these seven. However, depending on the college's requirements, implementing one or more of these writing strategies will certainly assist you in describing your learning.

## Strategy 1: How Do I Write a Detailed Description of My Learning?

- Use detailed examples to demonstrate that you have achieved the course outcome.
- Use terminology appropriately and in context.
- Describe your knowledge, skills, and abilities.
- Refer to supporting documentation in the description (see Chapter 11).

The following is a poorly written excerpt describing the learning outcome:

*For a public speaking course: Demonstrate the ability to use effective delivery techniques.*

Although this is only one of eight outcomes discussed in the narrative, this excerpt lacks detail about the student's skills and abilities related to the specific outcome.

*Every speech I gave for the United Way was an opportunity to use effective delivery techniques. I would arrive early and determine if I had a place to put my notes. I would survey where the audience would sit. There were several speeches that I used some pretty emotional details, which*

*I thought [were] overdone. I watched other speakers who just read from their notes when the[y] presented, gave the facts, and didn't even stay for questions. I even saw a person fall asleep. I knew my presentation skills were better. I never wanted an audience member to fall asleep when I spoke.*

This next excerpt is much improved and illustrates how to provide sufficient details to demonstrate the skills and abilities specific to the topic: effective delivery techniques. Key terms are also applied to the learning, enhancing the quality of the excerpt. You'll also notice the note at the end about "Document 5." This refers to the supporting documentation the learner included in her portfolio, which will be discussed further in Chapter 11.

*When I gave speeches about my company for the United Way, I learned how to improve my delivery. I arrived early to every event to make sure that I had the setup I needed. I preferred to use several flash cards with my notes so that I could keep my eyes on the audience. I remembered the lesson I learned from several years in Toastmasters. In Toastmasters, we were buzzed with a loud noise when we added fillers such as "uh." Those painful moments broke me of that annoying habit.*

*Since I am only five feet tall, I avoided standing behind big podiums, allowing the audience to see my gestures and me to see their faces. When I am nervous, I have the tendency to use too many gestures, so I tried to tone them down. I am generally a loud speaker and never had a problem with volume or enunciation.*

*One time I had a coworker time my speech, and what I thought was a five-minute speech was only three minutes. I needed to slow down and add pauses, which took practice. I even wrote "slow down" in large letters on my note cards.*

*Another aspect of delivery that was important in public speaking was appropriate dress. I always dressed professionally and more formally than casual business attire. I wanted to make sure that the audience took my message seriously. Finally, I didn't pace because there was often little room to move around, and I feared tripping on wires in high heels. I stood with my feet firmly planted and shoulder width apart. Paying attention to my delivery helped me keep the audience's attention and make a good impression. I received several commendations for my efforts (see Document 5: Letters).*

## Strategy 2: How Do I Write a Critical Incident Description to Demonstrate My Learning?

- Review Chapter 7's section on Kolb's model and critical incidents.
- Describe an incident. Answer the questions who, what, where, why, when, and how.
- Add a reflection on the learning.
- Conclude with an application of the learning.

Here is a narrative excerpt describing a critical incident related to customer service and support:

> As a technician in the air-conditioning service business, my service motto was "prevent disaster." In 1996, a large hotel in Las Vegas was planning to bring in a new piece of equipment to cool an exclusive part of the hotel. At my company, anything in Las Vegas that involved cooling a casino was top priority. I was working on the machine when I noticed a serious problem with one of the unit's large fans. I knew that if the machine wasn't running at the designated time, disaster was around the corner.
>
> I sat down and analyzed every possible solution to resolve the problem. This situation occurred on the weekend, so I had no support from the office. Assessing the need for quick action, I made all the appropriate calls to have the manufacturers ship parts overnight. When the packages arrived at the hotel, I worked extensively over the weekend to install the parts and bring the machine online before the deadline. Through the entire ordeal, I learned that by using critical thinking and applying fast action, I could find a solution. Over the subsequent six years I've had in customer service positions, I have used my skills in critical thinking and have applied them to avoid countless other customer disasters.

## Strategy 3: How Do I Describe Steps in My Learning?

- Demonstrate and describe learning progression from novice to expert.
- Personalize systematic instructions by adding colorful details and commentary. Identify and evaluate learning preferences. For instance, some students learn best from formal classroom instruction. Others learn by jumping in and making mistakes before consulting a manual or an expert.

- Summarize or condense the steps, if needed, to focus on advanced skill levels.

Describing stages or instructions can be useful for demonstrating learning in areas such as creating a work of art, conducting legal research, programming a computer, or resolving an electrical circuit problem.

Below is a narrative example of describing steps in learning related to the outcome:

*Ability to use HTML formatting codes to create basic Web pages. Again, we see references to supporting documentation in this example. The references are consistent and numbered chronologically as they appear in the narrative. Note: These references are here simply to demonstrate how you guide the assessor to your supporting documentation, which we will discuss further in Chapter 11. They are not references to examples of documentation to be found in this book.*

*Seven years ago, I completed a course on HTML (HyperText Markup Language) (see Document 1). Immediately, I had to use the < > buttons on the keyboard to create HTML opening and closing tags.*

*During this course, I learned how to create an HTML template on Windows Notepad (see Document 2). I started every page with <html> and ended with the corresponding closing tag </html>. I learned that if I didn't put the closing tag, I could mess up my document in a hurry. I learned how to play with the commands. As shown in Document 3, I used the appropriate tags to add a title (<title>) in bold (<bold>). Some tags didn't require a closing tag such as <hr>, which is a horizontal line. Document 4 shows how I wrote the HTML code for a hyperlink ("href" stands for hypertext reference): <a href="URL"> Text Here to Activate Link</a> as in <a href= "http://www.google.com">Link to Google</a>.*

*A similar pattern was used for creating e-mail links, as in: <a href ="mailto:timk@att.com">Contact me.</a> When I viewed the results through the browser, I could check my work. It helped to keep the browser window open for this purpose. . . . Using my basic template, I could move to a more advanced level where I created and formatted a table.*

Here we have the same learning outcome discussed step-by-step but in a competency statement format using columns.

| DESCRIPTION OF EXPERIENCE | LEARNING FROM EXPERIENCE | DOCUMENTATION |
|---|---|---|
| I know how to identify and use different HTML codes to format my documents. | I learned how to create opening and closing tags and view my results through a browser and make corrections. I learned how to properly format a header and footer. | Document 1—Course certificate in HTML from CompUSA (2008) |
| I can modify HTML documents using a text editor. | I learned formatting tags such as bold, underline, and italics. I learned HomeSite software. | Document 2—Sample of HTML using WordPad. Document 3—Sample using HomeSite Web-authoring tool |
| I can write Web pages that present information and graphics and provide hypertext links to other documents on the Internet. | I learned how to format tables, write hyperlinks, and insert graphics into my document. | Document 4—Sample of hyperlink code Document 5—Letter from employer |

# Strategy 4: How Do I Integrate Knowledge of Concepts in My Writing?

- Review Bloom's Taxonomy in Chapter 7.
- Demonstrate understanding of the concept by applying the knowledge to an experience.
- Cite relevant research and include a reference page of sources.

Narrative form related to methods of music/elementary education:

*Fraction proportion, pattern, division, and other math concepts repre-sent a few of the building blocks used in understanding music. Famous mathematicians such as Pythagoras (sixth century BC) first noted that the fractional pitch relationships in the lengths of strings have particular pat-terns in music (for example, half of a string makes the sound an octave higher). Another famous mathematician, Leonardo of Pisa (1200 BC), who was called Fibonacci, discovered a number pattern that works by adding two preceding numbers to find the third: 1, 1, 2, 3, 5, 8, 13, 21. The Fibo-nacci pattern has many applications to music, science, art, and literature.*

*In music, the pentatonic scale has five notes (2+3); the diatonic scale has eight notes (3+5). The Fibonacci numbers that children enjoyed discovering are the octaves—the eight white keys and the five black keys on the keyboard. By recognizing Fibonacci numbers in my music class, students enhanced their music and math skills.*

*Furthermore, to distinguish a waltz from a march, I taught my students math in order to recognize the meter signatures involved. After learning the math concepts, the children could move or dance in threes (3/4 time) or march in fours (4/4 time). The lyrics of the songs also convey math concepts. A song and accompanying activity that my third graders enjoyed was "Frog in the Bucket," an American song (see Document 5). When one out of the four children was inside the "bucket," the class would happily announce the fraction "1/4." Or, when two of four were in the "bucket," the student would say "2/4." . . . By analyzing the mathematical aspects of a song, the meter or time signatures, and the short and long sounds of the notes, I applied the standard knowledge of mathematics.*

Same excerpt using the column competency statement format.

| DESCRIPTION OF COMPETENCY | LEARNING FROM EXPERIENCE | DOCUMENTATION |
|---|---|---|
| Identify and teach mathematical concepts as they are employed in music. | I know and can teach children to discover Fibonacci numbers: octaves, the eight white keys, and the five black keys on the keyboard. | Documents 3–5 |
| | I know and can teach children to distinguish between a waltz and a march using movement and dance. | |
| | I know and can teach fractions using song and movement such as "Frog in the Bucket." | |

Here are some excerpts from a variety of subject areas illustrating even more ways to integrate concepts and experiences into your narrative or competency statement.

## Write a lead-in to a definition.

*One of the workshops I attended taught empathic listening skills, and we practiced the technique by dividing into pairs and trying role-playing. Empathic listening was defined by the speaker as . . .*

## List books or articles read. Include a reference page at the end of the narrative.

*During this period of reorganization, I read several books on managing change. Tom Peters (1987) writes, "Success will come to those who love chaos—constant change—not those who attempt to eliminate it." (p. 394) These books helped me understand that organizational stability was gone for good and I needed to adjust.*

## Describe information gained from an interview.

*I interviewed an owner of a salon, who gave me details about record-keeping methods and legal issues I might encounter. Also, I consulted an attorney who provided me with information such as . . .*

## Describe personal study.

*From living in other countries and appreciating other cultures, I observed that Latin and Asian cultures seemed more concerned about establishing a personal relationship before getting down to business. I applied this understanding when . . .*

# Strategy 5: How Do I Write Competency Statements?

Some colleges ask students to write competency statements instead of a narrative. Below are tips for writing competency statements.

- Describe knowledge, skills, and abilities used in a specific context.
- Identify actions that are observable and measurable.
  - □ Knowledge ("I know . . .")
  - □ Skills and ability ("I can do . . .")
  - □ Level of achievement ("At . . . level")
- Use strong verbs to describe learning. See lists below.
  - □ Knowledge and comprehension: classify, compare/contrast, conceptualize, define, describe, differentiate, explain, express, identify, illustrate, judge, know, label, list, name, paraphrase, practice, recall, review, select, state
  - □ Skill and ability: analyze, apply, assess, conceptualize, construct, create, demonstrate, design, develop, discuss, employ, examine, experiment, find, formulate, implement, invent, manage, plan, prepare, present, question, report, respond, solve, summarize, teach, use, write

Sample competency statements from a variety of subject areas:

- *I implemented the fourth-grade reading intervention goals and strategies to meet and exceed our individual literacy plan goals.*
- *I analyzed my golf swing on a videotape in order to improve my follow-through, lowering my average league score to 91.*
- *In order to accurately respond to client inquiries, I summarized and prepared bimonthly reports on current regulatory and industry changes that affected clients.*
- *After completing two seminars on using Westlaw for searches, I learned techniques to locate case laws and experimented with terms,connectors, and natural language to locate the maximum number of cases that were on point.*
- *As the assistant coordinator of public relations, I conceptualized and created a style guide for all grant writers in our organization in order to ensure a higher level of accuracy and consistency when applying for federal grants.*
- *I explained and applied the principles of ceramic processes such as glaze formulation, mold-making, and firing methods, at a level of ability that allows me to teach an advanced ceramics course at a local art studio.*
- *I applied my understanding of the seven-stage mediation process to help resolve a labor dispute at my workplace.*
- *I gained knowledge and practice in installing hardware components, such as hard drives, RAM, CD-ROMs, cables, and processors, in my job as a technical services technician.*
- *With one of my colleagues, I coauthored the training manual for new bookkeeping employees in the department (Document 2).*

## Strategy 6: How Do I Demonstrate My Problem-Solving Abilities?

- Demonstrate critical-thinking skills by analyzing a problem with sufficient detail.
- Describe and evaluate the solution.
- Describe your role in the process.

The following is an excerpt from the conclusion of a narrative related to records management.

*Document management is such a critical part of our business operation, and I have learned so much since I established and implemented this program.*

*The support of my general manager was necessary to begin the process. If I did not have the support of my management team, this project would not have succeeded. In addition, I established a records management team to assess our information system in order to identify and prioritize unmet needs or improvements to our system. I wanted to establish a records retention schedule that worked for our staff and find a user-friendly software program that would operate on our network and allow us to integrate electronic imaging.*

*The conference I attended and the listservs I consulted provided invaluable resources and answers to my questions. From this extensive process, I learned about communication and about my own skills and abilities. I confirmed to myself that my organizational skills and attention to detail allowed me to complete this project and establish an extremely effective company-wide system.*

*I received high praise from our management team, and the work that I did was reported to the board of directors. Our corporate attorney also praised my efforts; in fact, he told me that he has shared our information with many other corporate attorneys for use at the organizations they are representing. The culmination of this project was the presentation of the records management manual to our senior management team. This manual was used by all personnel and contained information on policies, procedures, and methods for our records management program.*

*Bottom line, it was satisfying to deliver a product that will be invaluable to my organization's future.*

## Strategy 7: How Do I Describe the Level of Learning I've Achieved?

There are several methods to describe your level of learning, as described below. Ultimately, however, the evaluator determines the level of learning achieved.

- Compare the level to the learning outcomes in a college course.

  *"I achieved a level of learning that is comparable to an introductory college photography course."*

- Compare the level to another source such as ACE recommendations.

  *"My level of learning is comparable to the ACE guide recommendation for training in Microsoft Word, Excel, PowerPoint, and Access. (ACE recommends one hour each in computer applications or information technology in the lower-division category.)"*

- Compare the level of learning to an outcome.

  *"I gained sufficient knowledge and experience to meet and exceed the learning described in the outcome—knowledge of literacy theories and practices."*

- Compare the level to other professionals in a similar context.

  *"My experience in the preparation and interpretation of financial and operating reports for several small businesses is comparable to the knowledge and ability required of an entry-level accountant."*

- Compare it to the level of learning needed to perform a specific job function.

  *"My ability is at a sufficient level to pass the examination and be employed as an on-call sign language interpreter for the state of California."*

- Compare the current level of learning to an earlier level of achievement.

  *"I worked as a C++ programmer for two years before receiving a promotion as wireless software developer."*

- Use supporting documentation to demonstrate the level of achievement or level of responsibility required for a position, such as:
  - Coursework or training records
  - Licenses or certifications
  - Letters from employers or experts in the field
  - Job descriptions
  - Performance reviews

## REVIEW

- There are many strategies for writing about learning. After researching and organizing your writing, follow your college's guidelines and write the best possible description of your learning.

- Do not exaggerate or underestimate your ability, but write an accurate, well supported, and complete demonstration of your learning.
- Using specific details, explanations of concepts, and strong competency statements helps build credibility.

## NEXT STEPS

1. Using your research and outline as a guide as well as the strategies covered in this chapter, write a narrative or competency statement to describe your learning.
2. Review the narrative or competency statements several times. adding sufficient details to demonstrate learning at the college level.
3. Edit your writing. Use an editing service, if available.

# Compiling Supporting Documentation and Submitting the Portfolio

*Note: The references to supporting documents used in this chapter are samples. The actual supporting documents are not included in this book.*

## What Is Supporting Documentation?

Supporting documentation, also known as documentation, artifacts, or exhibits, demonstrates or verifies your learning. Whitaker (1989) lists categories of documentation as:

- **Verification of accomplishment:** articles, meeting minutes, programs, reports, customer surveys, prizes
- **Testimony regarding competence:** performance evaluations, letters of verification, commendation letters
- **Learning products:** work samples, art objects, computer codes, written work or publications, Web sites, contracts, lesson plans
- **Certifications:** evidence of licenses, training records, ranks
- **Other direct evidence:** test scores, videos of performance
- **Descriptions:** job descriptions, membership requirements, syllabi (p. 56)

Whenever possible, provide duplicate copies of supporting documentation in your portfolio and keep the originals archived (this may not be possible with works of art). The supporting documentation can include both direct and indirect sources:

**Direct sources:** original work created, produced, written, designed, or composed by a student. Examples include reports, Web sites, computer designs, art objects, or videos of performances.

**Indirect sources:** documents produced by others that support or attest to a student's learning. Indirect sources might include certificates, meeting minutes, testimonies, performance evaluations, articles, contracts, or letters of verification.

Depending on the subject matter of the petition, you should use a combination of direct and indirect sources for supporting documentation.

## What Is the Purpose of Using Supporting Documentation?

1. Supporting documentation provides evidence of learning, the level of learning, and whether the learning is current. The supporting documentation should help evaluators make credit decisions. Therefore, supporting documentation provides evidence to back up your claims.

2. Supporting documentation helps colleges meet accreditation standards for assessment by showing that the evidence of the learning is accurate and that you are responsible for the work claimed. Verification letters should be from credible sources who have firsthand knowledge of the experiential learning you claim and should be written on letterhead.

3. Supporting documentation demonstrates your critical-thinking ability. Since compiling supporting documentation and obtaining letters of verification takes time and thought, it provides further evidence of your ability to think critically about your learning.

## How Do I Begin the Process of Gathering Supporting Documentation?

A good starting point is to consider what to gather and who could assist you. Often, finding one document leads to finding another. As you begin to gather materials, consider the following questions. After you have collected your documentation, complete the reflection activity in Box 11.1.

■ Do you have business cards, job descriptions, work products, or performance reviews from your job positions?

■ What on-the-job training or development have you had? Do you have records or certificates? Can you obtain records from a human resource department? Do you have outlines, programs, or certificates of completion from a course, workshop, seminar, conference, or training program? Did you obtain a government clearance or clear a criminal background check?

- Have you completed noncredit courses or independent studies? Have you completed courses that were not accepted for transfer credit (possibly due to accreditation standards)? Can you obtain transcripts or course descriptions?
- Have you participated in workshops, seminars, or conferences?
- Have you received awards, trophies, certificates, commendations, or letters of appreciation?
- Have you been licensed—for example, received a broker's, appraiser's, financial, contractor's, or real estate license?
- Do you have artistic or musical ability that can be supported with documentation or exhibits of paintings, jewelry, pottery, musical scores, programs, or photos?
- Do you have videos or CDs of performances such as dance, sign language interpretation, or speeches?
- Do you have photos of finished work, travel to other countries, missions, or volunteer trips?
- Have you volunteered extensively or developed hobbies that can be verified?
- Do you have documentation of your spiritual journey, such as notes from religious studies, training, or documents that verify your experience?
- From whom or where could you find copies of records?
- Who observed your work?
- Do you have a family member, friend, or coworker who could help you locate supporting documentation?
- Do you have the names of supervisors who can write letters of verification to include in your documentation?

## BOX 11.1   Reflection on Supporting Documentation

Describe the supporting documentation you've gathered. Why did you save each document or artifact? What are the best samples you could use to demonstrate your learning? Why are they the best?

# How Should I Select Supporting Documentation?

## Supporting documentation should be relevant to the subject matter.

The documents should relate to the learning outcomes described in the course or competency. The evaluator should be able to recognize the connection between the learning and the supporting documentation. When in doubt, ask your advisor whether a document verifies the claims to the learning. Weak examples of documentation include general articles or announcements without your name or a connection to your learning.

## Supporting documentation should be authentic.

The evidence used must be truthful representations of your learning. Box 11.2 lists some types of documents that you may be able to use. Letters of

## BOX 11.2  Types of Supporting Documentation

| | |
|---|---|
| Annotated bibliographies of reading | Licenses |
| Artwork | Manuals |
| Articles | Meeting minutes |
| Awards | Musical scores |
| Brochures | Patents |
| Budgets | Performance appraisals or reviews |
| Bulletin boards (photos) | Photos |
| Business cards | PowerPoint slides |
| Business correspondence | Presentation or meeting feedback forms |
| Certificates of training | Professional letters |
| Computer coding | Programs |
| Conference descriptions | Proposals |
| Contracts | Real estate records |
| Corporate announcements | Reports |
| Creative writing (such as plays, poems, and stories) | Software programs |
| Curricula and lesson plans | Spreadsheets |
| Graphics | Surveys |
| Job descriptions | Video or audio tape |
| Letters from satisfied customers | Web sites |
| Letters of verification of the learning | Workshop descriptions |
| | Writing |

verification can testify that your produced the work alone or with a team, as well as the level of knowledge, skills, and abilities involved. Always be open and honest about your contributions to projects.

**Supporting documentation should represent the best samples.**

When selecting supporting documentation, quality is more important than quantity. For instance, one or two of the best samples of written work, such as lesson plans, newsletters, or computer codes, are better than multiple samples. If, for example, you wrote a manual, several sample pages and a letter of verification attesting to your authorship would be sufficient.

When choosing samples, always keep the audience in mind. Evaluators are busy and not impressed when students pad the portfolio with irrelevant or redundant samples. Remember that one document may demonstrate learning in a number of areas and can be cross-referenced in the narrative or competency statements. "Don't overwhelm me by padding the portfolio with extraneous documents," said one evaluator.

# What Are Letters of Verification?

A letter of verification provides validation of your knowledge, skills, and abilities related to the areas being petitioned in the portfolio. The author of the letter must have firsthand knowledge of your work and level of expertise. The letter verifies the learning, so it differs from a letter of appreciation or commendation. In addition, the letter should be written by a reliable and credible source, such as an employer or expert. The letter should not be written by a friend or family member. The letter of verification is typically written on letterhead and signed by the author.

# What Are Some Tips for Requesting Letters of Verification?

Start the process of soliciting letters early and monitor your requests using a calendar or checklist with the date of each request and the date received. One effective way to request letters is to call the writer first, and then follow up with an e-mail detailing the specifics of the purpose and necessary contents of the requested letter. Box 11.3 describes what should be included in a letter of verification. Box 11.4 shows a letter of verification request by e-mail.

## BOX 11.3   Letters of Verification

A high-quality letter of verification includes:

1. Author's credentials, relationship to the student, and dates observed.
2. Description of the "duties, responsibilities, and tasks involved in the experiential learning under consideration" (Whitaker, 1989, p. 58).
3. Summary or list of the learning (knowledge, skills, and abilities) achieved as a result of performing these duties.
4. Statement that attests to the performance level based on one or more of the following factors:

   - Level of learning demonstrated compared to others in a known reference group (e.g., average, above average, superior)
   - Level of development observed (e.g., progress from novice to expert)
   - Level of performance comparable to a college-level course (if needed, students can provide information for the writer on the course or competencies under consideration)
   - Level of transferability of the skills (i.e., highly transferable skills would mean the skill sets acquired would easily transfer to other jobs or projects)

5. The letter should be signed, dated, and printed on letterhead.


## BOX 11.4   Sample Letter of Verification Request by E-mail

Subject line: Letter needed by 11/22

Dear _____

As a follow-up to our conversation, I am requesting a verification letter to include in my prior learning portfolio. The purpose of the letter is to verify my experiential learning and the level of learning I achieved in the areas described below.

(continued)

Please include the following elements in the letter:

1. State your title, relationship to me, and dates observed. For reference, you supervised my work at the company from 7/2010–8/2011.

2. Provide a short description of the duties I performed alone or as part of a team. Attest that I worked as a customer service assistant and then a customer services team leader.

3. Provide a brief summary of the knowledge, skills, and abilities I demonstrated in the following areas: (name competencies associated with the coursework being petitioned).

4. Attest to the level at which I performed these competencies (average, above average, superior). Attest to the level of my competency compared to a lower-division course. I am petitioning for credits toward my elective category for the degree.

5. Include any other statements that would help an evaluator determine what skills I demonstrated when I performed as a team leader.

6. The letter should be signed, dated, and printed on letterhead.

Please mail the letter to me at (provide address), or I will pick up the letter on (date).

Thank you in advance for your help as I pursue my educational goal of achieving my bachelor's degree in business administration. Please e-mail or phone me with any questions.

Sincerely,

(Name, title, address, e-mail address, phone number)

# What Is a Statement of Authenticity?

A statement of authenticity attests to the validity of the claim. There are two types of statements of authenticity:

1. Your signature, indicating that you are responsible for the work presented and that all supporting documentation is an accurate and true representation.

2. A statement on letterhead by another person who testifies that the work presented is an accurate and true representation of your work. In cases where you worked on a project as part of a team, the statement indicates your level of contribution.

## What Materials Are Useful for Compiling Supporting Documentation?

Follow your college's guidelines. The following are some materials typically used by portfolio students:

1. Archival storage for originals: For e-portfolios, make sure to back up all of your files on a CD-ROM, flash drive, or some other storage device in addition to your hard drive. This way, if anything happens to your computer, you will still be able to retrieve these very important files. Similarly, store hard copies of documentation safely and in an organized manner using a filing system, a binder, or a storage box. Do not laminate documents.
2. Binder: Use a three-ring binder. If the portfolio is divided by subject matter, you can use several small three-ring binders. D-ring binders help supporting documentation lay flat. Zippered binders are best if including supporting documentation such as a CD-ROM.
3. Clear sheet protectors (if required by the college).
4. Section dividers or tabs.
5. Double sided tape.
6. Labels.
7. Yellow highlighter: If needed, use a yellow highlighter or other method to draw attention to the sentences or sections of a document that are relevant to the learning outcomes. For example, a sentence in a performance review can be highlighted to draw focus to the section that verifies your skills and abilities.

Avoid Sticky notes, paper clips, or anything that could fall off the pages of the portfolio.

## What Are Some Tips for Compiling Supporting Documentation?

Here is some advice from Amy Dressel-Martin of Dressel-Martin MediaWorks Inc. on preparing professional-looking supporting documentation.

- Use either bold or underlining for captions; don't mix the two.
- Use easy-to-read fonts such as Times or Times New Roman.
- Use a consistent format in the paper, type, style, and headings you use.
- Use a high-quality printer or copier to print out or make copies of documents. If needed, trim and use correction fluid to clean up documents before copying.
- Use black ink.
- Check for spelling and grammatical errors.
- Use plastic sleeves, if allowed. Use non-glare sleeves, if available.
- Keep the pages clean and uncluttered, placing only one or two items on a page.
- Use one-inch margins on pages.
- Use high-quality white paper for documents such as résumés.
- Place photos on the left side of the page and put captions on the right, or center the caption and photo on the page.
- Clip and photocopy articles with the dateline and publication intact on the first page of the article, or cut the dateline and publication and tape the information on top of the page with the article below before copying.
- Avoid using clip art or stickers (exception: graphic artist or teacher education portfolio).

## How Do I Organize and Reference My Supporting Documentation?

Prepare an index to documents on a separate page that lists all sources of documentations. If needed, provide an explanation if a caption does not describe the document. Normally, supporting documentation is numbered in the order discussed in the narrative or competency statement. It can also be listed thematically or chronologically. Commonly, students use tabs or section dividers so evaluators can easily turn to the correct supporting documentation. When referencing supporting documentation in a narrative or competency statement, put the parenthesis before the final punctuation in a sentence, as follows:

- *I created a bulletin board for social studies students to provide a visual representation of the timeline of events (see photo in Document 3).*
- *In the next two positions, I wrote performance evaluations for my employees (refer to sample 4.1 and 4.2 and verification letter in Document 5).*

- *I revised the human resource benefits publication several times and received a commendation from my employer for my efforts (refer to Document 5).*

# What Are Captions, and How Do I Write Effective Ones?

Captions provide brief explanations of the documents. A good caption incorporates the "five Ws": who, what, why, where, and when. If the process of creating the supporting documentation is particularly relevant, you could add an explanation of "how." Effective captions are accurate and spelled correctly. If there are several items on a page or people in a photo, the caption should identify the items from left to right.

Depending on the college's requirements, captions can be included on an index page or typed and printed on labels and adhered to the copies of the documents or the plastic sheet protectors. If needed, the caption can provide an explanation of the relevance of the document to a specific learning outcome. In addition, captions can be used to show evidence of improvement or steps taken to gain competency. The sample captions in Box 11.5 show how adding specifics can make captions more useful for the evaluators.

## BOX 11.5   Writing Captions

*Weak: The photo above shows me accepting an award.*

Strong: Document 3. The photo (above) was taken in September of 2011 when I received an award from the Nonprofit Center of Colorado for my work in planning, writing, and producing a resource directory.

*Weak: Certificate in JavaScript.*

Strong: Supporting documentation 8 and 9. In November of 2009, I attended a two-week intensive course on Java programming sponsored by the Computer Training Institute and attended by myself and employees of Systems, Inc. The course description and course topics, shown to the right, were retrieved and printed from the Computer Training Institute's Web site.

(continued)

> *Weak: Before and after samples.*
>
> Strong: Supporting documentation 6 and 7—before and after samples of business writing.
>
> *Weak:* The document on the left side of the page is an excerpt from the company request document I wrote in September of 2010 (names blacked out to protect privacy). This written request was too lengthy and disorganized.
>
> Strong: The document on the right, which I wrote in November of 2011, demonstrates the competencies I gained in business writing, including attention to the audience, clear organization, and proper editing.

## How Many Pieces of Supporting Documentation Do I Need?

The number depends on the college's requirements and the subject matter. For example, teacher education portfolios may require a variety of supporting documentation like letters, lesson plans, student papers, and training records. Many schools recommend approximately five pieces of supporting documentation for each three-credit course being petitioned. In all cases, "excessive documentation, attractively presented, should not compensate for poor performance in assessment." (Whitaker, 1989, p. 58).

## What If I Am Having Trouble Locating Supporting Documentation?

First, if you have the learning, write a thorough narrative or competency statement that attests with enough detail to your knowledge, skills, and abilities. In addition, while writing the narrative or competency statements, you may get ideas for potential supporting documentation and sources that will verify your learning, such as business cards, brochures, job descriptions, or certificates.

Second, you may be able to find current e-mail addresses or contact information for former employers by using Internet search engines, free online directories, or social and professional networking sites in order to request letters of verification.

Third, in some instances, you can reproduce your original work. For instance, if you cannot locate the outline for a speech given several years earlier, you could recreate the outline. Indirect documentation such as job descriptions, flyers, or a letter of verification could validate that you presented the speech.

Fourth, in cases where information is proprietary, you should include an explanation about why the document is not included or information is blacked out (see the following questions on proprietary information).

Fifth, if the learning is not verifiable with supporting documentation, consider other assessment methods. It is always advisable to discuss these challenges with a portfolio specialist.

## Are the Contents of My Portfolio Kept Confidential?

The portfolio contents will only be reviewed by a faculty member and the evaluator(s). Portfolio contents are not shared with the general public without your consent. If you're concerned, ask the college for their confidentiality statement or policy on confidentiality. Portfolios are not shared with other students unless you provide a written release. Even so, personal information and company names are generally blacked out before the contents are shown to other students. You should always take the necessary precautions when using proprietary information (see next question).

## What Is Proprietary Information and How Do I Protect Any I Have in My Supporting Documentation?

Propriety information is "material and information relating to or associated with a company's products, business, or activities, including, but not limited to, financial information; data or statements; trade secrets; product research and development; existing and future product designs and performance specifications; marketing plans or techniques; schematics; client lists; computer programs; processes; and know-how that has been clearly identified and properly marked by the company as proprietary information, trade secrets, or company confidential information" (ATIS, 2011).

### Protecting Proprietary Information

- Obtain permission to use any documents that have been identified as proprietary information, trade secrets, or company confidential information.
- Black out proprietary information such as names, dates, e-mails, and project findings on documents by using a black marker or white-out tape, and then photocopying the document.

- Black out faces of children in classroom settings, if advised, to protect privacy.
- Find indirect sources that do not reveal proprietary information.
- Write captions to explain the circumstances.
- Obtain a letter, if needed, to verify the authenticity of the work.

# What Is an E-Portfolio and How Does It Work?

Some colleges provide password-protected **electronic portfolios**—also known as e-portfolios, Webfolios, or digital portfolios—which are commonly used as career portfolios, to demonstrate writing, or to show competencies in teacher education programs. Batson (2002) defines an electronic portfolio as a "dynamic Web site that interfaces with a database of student work artifacts" (para. 8).

## Advantages of Using an E-Portfolio

- **Easy Storage and Portability.** You can upload and store documents to an e-portfolio platform and access your portfolio from any Internet location.
- **Space.** Depending on the amount of storage space, you can add scanned documents, audio, video clips, slide presentations, and graphics. Determine what the storage capacity is, and if needed, find free sites that can help compress documents like images into small sizes.
- **Visual and Oral Elements.** You can use a digital camera or video camera to capture photographic images or movies, then upload them to the e-portfolio platform. Or, you might upload videos to a Web site (such as YouTube.com) and link to the site.
- **Sharing.** On most e-portfolio platforms, you can invite others to view your portfolio contents. In order to see your documents, viewers must be on a computer that has the proper software.
- **Loading.** Loading word processing documents on an e-portfolio site is not difficult; in fact, it is a similar process to adding attachments to an e-mail.
- **Reflection.** An e-portfolio without reflection is incomplete. It is not enough to load documents on a site or arrange the electronic portfolio for visual appeal. The portfolio must demonstrate reflection on the learning and professional development.
- **Version Control.** Most electronic portfolio platforms allow users to publish different versions of a portfolio, giving you the ability to restrict or

allow access to specific documents depending on the viewer. The user provides corresponding access information via e-mail to the intended viewer.

- **Growth.** The e-portfolio is student-owned and can be a catalyst for documenting goals and achievements for many years. Over time, you can see changes in your level of learning.

## Challenges to Using an E-Portfolio

- **Planning.** Like any project, loading an electronic portfolio requires planning and forethought. The portfolio should represent thoughtfully selected representations of your learning. More is not necessarily better, and in fact, too many documents may detract from the quality elements of the e-portfolio. Likewise, too many "bells and whistles" can be distracting to an assessor.

- **Fees.** Some colleges provide their own electronic portfolio platforms free of charge to students; other e-portfolio platforms may require a fee.

- **Learning Curve.** Although most electronic portfolio platforms are intuitive, there may be a learning curve. Some sites have videos or help menus to get you started. In general, you will not need some of the advanced Web interfaces that require extensive training on the tool.

- **Scanning Quality.** Documents that are difficult to decipher when scanned may require a caption to explain the contents.

- **Assessor's Capabilities.** Always consider the needs and software capabilities of the evaluators when building an electronic portfolio. Do not upload a document to your e-portfolio that cannot be downloaded by the assessor.

- **Confidentiality.** As with any document housed on the Web, there can be security breaches. A password-protected site may provide a level of security, but it is not a guarantee of absolute privacy. If you are concerned about highly confidential items, discuss your concerns with the college. Some company information, if disclosed, could harm you, a colleague, or an employer, so using due diligence in protecting privacy is critical.

- **Information Overload.** The portfolio should be simple to navigate and consistent in layout. Always recheck your e-portfolio to make sure that items are organized logically and loaded properly. The assessor of a portfolio will have limited time; therefore, a consistent, simple design is best. The contents should be named in a clear, straightforward manner so that the elements are evident. If in doubt, have several viewers access your portfolio and watch how they navigate your site to determine if the documents are clearly labeled and easy to access.

- **Back Up All Your Documents.** Create and archive supporting documentation in electronic form. **Digitize** paper documents if possible. Use a portable storage device or organize supporting documentation in folders and subfolders on a hard drive.
- **Time Management.** When creating your e-portfolio, you may be tempted to spend time on design elements like digital scrapbooking, digital storytelling, or other tools. You should spend the most time on the critical elements that are being assessed. Certainly, other digital elements can be used and added later.
- **Additional Resource.** Visit Dr. Helen Barrett's interactive Web site at http://www.electronicportfolios.org for more information on electronic portfolios and digital storytelling.

## Tip from a Student:

*"First, I prepared my documents for the e-portfolio and saved them in a folder on my computer. The best advice I have is to use an easy-to-identify name when saving documents so you can find them when you are ready to load your e-portfolio. Also, since I had several drafts of my learning narrative, I clearly named and saved the most current version. Next, I set up my e-portfolio from a template provided by the college. I became familiar with the template, tabs, and navigation to see where I had to upload my documents. I printed the step-by-step instructions and checked each step when it was completed. Finally, I uploaded and wrote captions for each document and gave permission to the college to view the e-portfolio for assessment. Since I had all my documents ready, it was easy to upload my e-portfolio contents."*

## Perspective from an E-Portfolio Service Provider:

*"Our users have taught us that portfolios can be successfully used in a wider range of areas than expected, presenting many new opportunities. Individual users appreciate the ability to archive their best works in one place and then choose to share them with specific groups for a variety of purposes. When beginning a portfolio project we have found that it is very helpful to ask the question: 'What would define success?' Flexible portfolio systems like iWebfolio (http://www.iwebfolio.com) can support broad use across a wide range of personal, academic, and workforce purposes. When the purpose of the portfolio is clear, users have a richer*

*and more useful experience. We expect the use of portfolios to grow dramatically over the next few years."*

Dr. David Raney, Nuventive CEO

## What Are Some Tips for Submitting My Portfolio?

1. Create a submission checklist of items that you will include in your portfolio—or use one that the college has provided. Recheck that all the contents are included. It is easy to leave out an item such as a letter of validation that hasn't arrived.
2. Always keep backup copies of every item in the portfolio in an archive.
3. Submit the portfolio by the deadline.
4. Check that the contents are edited, organized, and professional-looking, but don't overdo the formatting. Remember that the purpose of your portfolio is to demonstrate learning. It can be tempting to spend too much time arranging supporting documentation or creating graphics while neglecting to prepare high-quality narratives or competency statements.

## Using Your Portfolio for Career Development

As you know, one of the reasons for creating a portfolio is to request college-level credit; however, there are additional advantages you should also consider. Many students keep building their electronic portfolios and customize them for career planning and development.

1. **Use the portfolio in a job interview.** Generally, interviewers are short on time, so they may not want to see your entire portfolio; however, now that you have all of your documents in one place that is easily accessible from the Internet, you'll have no problem quickly selecting a document to show a potential employer. The idea is to ask the interviewer if he or she would like to see the document first. Then select, show, and discuss the item with the interviewer. Your portfolio can provide validation of the competencies you have gained in your experiences.
2. **Use the portfolio for a job change or promotion.** You might continue to add documents to your portfolio so that when you are preparing for a job change or a promotion, you can quickly access information on your latest accomplishments.

3. **Use the portfolio to save copies as a backup.** Sometimes students move or have a change in their work or military assignment, and they can easily lose documents. The portfolio is great as a backup and storage repository. Of course, you should always keep the original documents in a safe place.

## Creating Your Future

Utilize the prior learning portfolio and the prior learning assessment process to help you create your own future. When you create a prior learning portfolio, you are creating a record of your personal and professional development. Use the portfolio process for personal reflection on your career. In this rapidly changing work world, reflection is imperative because it helps you make sound career and educational decisions. The portfolio will help you assess where you've been, where you are now, and where you want to go. Many portfolio students successfully utilize the process to recognize how they could build on the past, reflecting on what pieces were relevant or not to their long-term career planning. The portfolio process will inevitably help you determine threads and patterns of knowledge you have gained and any skills you may need for future endeavors. Use this opportunity to create *your* own future.

## Adult Learner Profiles

Appendices 5–10 include excerpts and examples of Tim and Maria's portfolio work. Take some time to look at these samples, as they will give you good ideas for compiling your own portfolio.

Appendix 5 shows Tim's table of contents and supporting documentation index. Notice how Tim carefully blacked out proprietary information and received permission from his boss to use the material.

Appendix 6 illustrates Maria's course research for an Intro to Communication course.

Appendix 7 is an excerpt from Maria's narrative for the Intro to Communication course and includes a cover sheet and statement of authenticity.

Appendix 8 takes the same information from Maria's narrative and presents it in the three-column format for a competency statement.

Appendix 9 is an example of a letter of verification Maria requested to demonstrate and validate her communication skills.

Lastly, Appendix 10 includes an excerpt from the evaluation of Maria's portfolio.

# Review

- Finding the best supporting documentation to demonstrate your learning requires critical thinking.
- Letters are a form of documentation used to verify that the learning has taken place.
- Captions help explain the nature of your supporting documents as well as the reasons for their inclusion.
- Take appropriate measures to protect proprietary information.
- When using an electronic portfolio, supporting documentation can be scanned and uploaded.

# Next Steps

1. Locate, arrange, and provide captions for supporting documentation.
2. Follow the requirements for submitting the portfolio and paying the assessment fees, if any.

# Final Remarks

Many adult students who return to school have survived the threats of downsizing and restructuring. They've recognized the need for retraining or a degree, but are fearful about returning to school. Through prior learning assessment, students gain confidence in their ability to perform at the college level. In addition, they are able to earn credit for their skills, knowledge, and abilities.

Keep in mind these important points when undertaking the PLA process:

- Determine a goal and make an academic plan.
- Receive information and guidance on the college's methods and policies for the assessment of prior learning.
- Reflect during and after experiences.
- Appreciate how writing about learning leads to new learning.
- Budget time to fully benefit from assessment methods such as portfolio development.

College students in their 70s, 80s, even 90s are finding pleasure in a return to school (see Box 11.6). Learning does not stop in high school, or even at midlife. Learning is a lifelong activity.

## Box 11.6 A Little Inspiration

In 2007, Nola Ochs became the world's oldest college grad at the age of 95! Three years later, Nola graduated with her master's degree! But in May of 2011, her title of oldest college graduate was usurped by 99-year-old Leo Plass, who received his associate's degree from Eastern Oregon University in Le Grande, Oregon! Looking back on *your* accomplishments in life, what are you proud of?

**All of your learning is valuable, and it's NEVER too late to go to college!**

## Note from the Author

Receiving credit through prior learning assessment is an effective catalyst for students who are determined to complete a college degree. As of this date, "Andrew" has completed his doctorate and is teaching at a university. "Tim" received the raise he desired, and "Maria" is now close to completing her bachelor's degree and teacher's licensure.

Chris will be discharged from the military in the fall. She has been accepted to the college of her choice starting in the spring semester, knowing the college has a rigorous PLA program and will accept all her CLEP and DSST exam credits. This coming fall, she will enroll in the online PLA course and work with her advisor to schedule on-campus courses for the spring. She has prepared well for her college experience.

I hope that this book will inspire other students to earn college credit for what they know.

—Janet Colvin

## RESOURCE

ACE (2008). Mapping new directions:  Higher Education for older adults. Retrieved from http://www.acenet.edu/Content/NavigationMenu/ProgramsServices/CLLL/Reinvesting/MapDirections.pdf

# Appendices

# Finding Institutions That Offer Prior Learning Assessment

Students can use several methods for locating institutions that offer prior learning assessment.

1. Find a college or university that offers the program or major you are seeking.
2. Go to the college's Web site and use the search function to locate "prior learning assessment. You can also try the search term "adult learners." Often prior learning assessment is mentioned in the instructions for the admissions process.
3. You can also call a college or university to find out if it offers prior learning assessment. For instance:
   - Andrew enrolled in the adult learning program at his local college and found out about prior learning assessment during the admissions process.
   - Tim was directed to the testing office and then to the department for adult learner services.
   - Maria initially inquired at a four-year institution and was referred to the local community college.
     Offices that may be able to help you get the information you need include Admissions, Continuing Studies, Veteran's Affairs, Student Services, among others.
4. If available, use e-mail to reply to the "Contact Us" feature on a school's (or adult learning program's) Web site to inquire about prior learning assessment options.
5. Ask an admissions representative or advisor at the college if prior learning assessment services are available.
6. If a college does not offer a portfolio assessment program, find out if it will accept transfer credits earned through prior learning assessment from another institution. Often colleges have agreements with other local colleges that provide portfolio assessment programs. Students

may have to register for a portfolio or prior learning assessment course through the partnering institution and then transfer the credit.

7.  Search for adult learning programs on the Internet or use one of the key words or phrases listed below:
    - Prior learning assessment
    - Credit options
    - Assessment of prior learning
    - Learning from experience
    - Challenge exams
    - Credit by examination
    - Testing
    - Admissions
    - Experiential learning
    - Adult learning or professional studies

    Departments that may house prior learning assessment services:
    - Advising
    - Admissions
    - Student services
    - Registrar
    - Testing
    - Prior learning assessment services
    - Career counseling

The assessment of prior learning may be listed under a number of names:

- Prior Learning Assessment (PLA)
- Prior Learning Assessment and Recognition (PLAR—Canadian)
- Assessment of Prior Learning or Flexible Assessment (APL—UK)
- Recognition of Prior Learning (RPL—Australian and South African)
- Assessment and Recognition of Prior Learning and Experience (ARPLE)
- Assessment of Prior Certified Learning (APCL)
- Accreditation of Prior Experiential Learning (APEL)
- Credit for Prior Learning (CPL)

To locate colleges that offer CLEP and DSST testing sites, visit:

- CLEP @ http://clep.collegeboard.com
- DSST @ http://www.getcollegecredit.com

To locate colleges that recognize ACE credit recommendations, visit:
- http://www.acenet.edu

# Prior Learning Inventory

Adult learners often have a variety of learning experiences, including college credit courses, workshops and seminars, certifications, and workplace learning. The purpose of the prior learning inventory is to list your experiences, training, and learning competencies that may be useful for assessment planning. This information will be helpful for planning your education as well as beginning to determine your college-level learning and what methods of prior learning assessment to explore. The information gathered for this process will help you organize your experiences and learning. This information will also help an academic advisor or prior learning specialist assist you in developing an effective educational plan. If you decide to create a portfolio, the information will be essential for developing the contents.

## Create a Folder

Start by creating a folder in a location on your computer that is easy to access or use a paper filing system. As you complete the prior learning inventory and, subsequently, the exercises in this book, save each document in this folder. Label your folder "Prior Learning Inventory" or a similar name that is easy to identify.

The documents you save in your folder include:

Part 1: Prior Learning Inventory. An inventory of your experiences.
Part 2: List of Skills. A list of the general skills and categories that match your learning.
Part 3: Competencies. A list of the competencies you have obtained from your experience.

On the following pages are instructions to guide you through the process of creating these documents. Let's get started!

# PART 1    Prior Learning Inventory

Instructions:

1. State your experiences in each of the areas of possible learning.
2. For each experience, add details, including dates (can be approximate), type of experience, and a brief description.
3. Skip sections that do not apply.
4. Update your inventory as needed.

Categories:

1. Name and identification information
   *Include: name, address, work and home phone numbers, e-mail address(es), fax number, student ID or Social Security number*
2. High school information
   *Include: name of school, dates of attendance, type of degree (diploma or GED)*
3. Education after high school
   *Include: dates, name of school, Web site, concentration or types of courses completed*
4. Military service
   *Include: branch, date entered, date discharged, rank*
   *Optional: military training, schools, type/length of training, occupational specialty, brief description of types of military assignments*
5. Languages
   *Include: language, fluency level (beginning, advanced), spoken or written (or both)*
6. Professional training
   (non-credit courses and independent studies, distance courses, workshops, seminars and conferences, training programs, certifications or examinations passed)
   *Include: dates, title, school or sponsor, type of training*
7. Employment history
   *Include: dates, company name, type of business, job titles, job duties, location*
   *Optional: insert the section of your résumé that lists employment history (include supervisors' names, addresses, e-mail addresses)*
8. Professional societies or organizations
   *Include: dates, names, membership held, offices held, committees, service*

(continued)

9. Original work
   (written documents such as original reports, articles, grants, technical manuals, marketing materials, copyrights, Web sites, and intranets prepared either by you or a team)
   *Include: dates, companies, brief description*
10. Computer or technical expertise
    *Include: dates, type of training, software skills, computer languages, level of mastery (beginning, intermediate, advanced)*
11. Civic or political organizations or activities
    *Include: dates, organizations, brief descriptions of duties*
12. Volunteer activities
    *Include: dates, organizations, brief descriptions of duties*
13. Sports and recreational pursuits
    *Include: dates, type, level of expertise, training received*
14. Artistic pursuits
    (artistic ability and knowledge, skills, appreciation of the arts)
    *Include: dates, type, brief description of artistic works or artist's portfolio*
15. History, cultural, or regional studies
    (knowledge of history, travel, cultures, regions, anthropology, or geography)
    *Include: dates, type, brief descriptions*
16. Religious and spiritual activities
    (training, memberships, reading, courses, small groups, retreats, committees served, missions, self-help programs, or recovery programs)
    *Include: dates, sponsor, brief descriptions*
17. Accomplishments
    (inventions or patents, commendations, honors or promotions, trophies, letters of appreciation, or recognitions)
    *Include: dates, organization, brief descriptions*

18. Transcript checklist
    List transcripts and records requested. Include college transcripts, ACE, and military records (see Chapter 5 for more details).
    *Include: type of transcript, date requested*

The length of your learning inventory will depend on the amount of formal and informal training or learning you have experienced.

Below is a sample of what a learning inventory might look like. Create a new row for each area of learning.

| DATES | PLACE | TITLE OR TYPE (AS APPLICABLE) | LEARNING HISTORY SUPPORTING DOCUMENTATION |
|---|---|---|---|
| **_List of Formal Learning_** | | | |
| List the dates or approximate date ranges here. | Name the location: colleges, military, training organizations, testing type, or indicate "self-directed learning." | College credit earned. Title of course and number of credits earned.<br><br>College-level testing (e.g., CLEP or DSST). Title of exam and number of credits.<br><br>Types of independent study.<br><br>Types of training. | Indicate "yes" if you can obtain a copy of a transcript or certificate that supports the completion of this learning. |
| **_List of Informal Learning_** | | | |
| List the dates or approximate date ranges here. | Name the location: the workplace or organization that served as the parent umbrella to your learning. | Job title held, non-certified workplace training.<br><br>Knowledge, skills, and abilities that you acquired in this environment. | Indicate "yes" if you have any documents available that might support the learning from this environment. |

# PART 2  General Categories

Now that you've created an inventory of your learning experiences, take a look at each area of learning you listed and brainstorm the general categories that match. You can use the list provided below to help generate ideas.

| | | |
|---|---|---|
| Accounting | Graphics | Project management |
| Advertising | History | Public relations |
| Art | Hotel | Public speaking |
| Broadcasting | Hospitality | Purchasing |
| Business | Horticulture | Quality control |
| Business software | Human resources | Real estate |
| Buying | Human services | Retail |
| Communication | Insurance | Research |
| Computer | Intercultural skills | Safety |
|    programming | Interpersonal skills | Sales |
| Conflict resolution | Interviewing | Science |
| Construction | Investigation | Social work |
| Counseling | Journalism | Small business |
| Customer service | Labor relations | Spirituality |
| Database | Language | Sports |
|    management | Law | Supervision |
| Design | Leadership | Team-building |
| Drafting | Literacy | Technical support |
| Education | Managing | Telecommunication |
| Economics | Marketing | Trade |
| Engineering | Medicine | Training |
| Environmental | Music | Volunteer work |
|    science | Nutrition | Web design |
| Finance | Nonprofit | Writing |
| Fire science | Office administration | Other _____ |
| Fundraising | Police training | |

# PART 3    Skills and Competencies

For each category you applied to your learning in Part 2, specify the skills and competencies you obtained. Many skills, such as managing projects, involve both people and data.

| PEOPLE SKILLS | INFORMATION/ DATA SKILLS | DOING SKILLS |
|---|---|---|
| Appreciating (diversity, styles, differences) | Analyzing | Adjusting |
| Coaching | Applying | Assembling |
| Communicating | Budgeting | Building |
| Consulting | Clarifying | Calculating |
| Coordinating | Composing | Coding |
| Creating | Computing | Completing tasks |
| Delegating | Conceptualizing | Constructing |
| Evaluating | Data collecting | Creating (visual arts) |
| Facilitating | Decision making | Delivering |
| Handling conflict | Developing ideas | Demonstrating |
| Helping | Editing | Designing |
| Leading | Estimating | Driving/operating |
| Listening | Evaluating | Engineering |
| Managing conflict | Examining | Growing |
| Mediating | Formulating | Handling |
| Mentoring | Gathering | Inventing |
| Mobilizing | Handling logistics | Making things |
| Motivating | Investigating | Manipulating |
| Negotiating | Learning | Manufacturing |
| Performing | Managing projects | Operating equipment |
| Presenting | Observing | Producing |
| Recruiting | Organizing | Repairing |
| Relaying information | Problem solving | Tuning |
| Satisfying customers | Reading for information | Using numbers, software programs, tools, materials |
| Selling | Reporting | Working with |
| Supervising | Researching | _____ |
| Teaching | Scheduling tasks | |
| Team-building | Setting procedures | |
| Training | Sorting | |
| Understanding | Strategizing | |
| | Streamlining | |
| | Structuring | |
| | Studying | |
| | Supplying | |
| | Synthesizing | |
| | Testing quality | |
| | Visualizing | |
| | Writing | |

Another great way to discover specific skills you may have overlooked is to use O*Net Online. O*Net Online is the U.S. Department of Labor's compiled database of job descriptions and detailed work activities. Use this Web site as an aid in creating your learning inventory and in reminding yourself of all the things you know!

- Go to O*Net Online **at http://www.onetonline.org/**.
- See the Occupation Search box.
- Enter keywords of area(s) where you have experience (e.g., customer service, accounting, teaching, welding).
- Find specific words and sentences that may assist you to describe your learning.
- Save or print a few of the results to assist you when writing your learning inventory.
- Now click on the Advanced Search option.
- Choose the Tools and Technology search option.
- Enter specific tools or software you know to find related occupations that need your skills.

For U.S. schools, accreditation is recognized by the Council on Higher Education Accreditation (CHEA), which is online at www.chea.org.

The six regional accrediting institutions include:

- Middle State Association of Colleges and Schools @ http://www.msache.org
- New England Association of Schools and Colleges @ http://www.neasc.org
- North Central Association of Colleges and Schools @ http://www.ncacihe.org
- Northwest Association of Schools and Colleges @ http://www.cocnasc.org
- Southern Association of Colleges and Schools @ http://www.sacs.org
- Western Association of Schools and Colleges @ http://www.wascweb.org

Schools in Great Britain and the British Commonwealth must be members of the Association of Commonwealth Universities and have a listing in the Commonwealth Universities Yearbook.

Schools in Australia must be recognized by the Australian Qualifications Framework.

Schools not covered by the aforementioned accrediting bodies must be in either the World Education Series, published by Projects for International Education Research (PIER), or in the Country Series, published by Australia's National Office for Overseas Skills Recognition.

The book *Bears' Guide to Earning Degrees* by Distance Learning, now in its 16th edition (2006), offers a wealth of information utilizing the generally accepted accrediting principles (GAAP) to determine which schools offering distance learning are accredited. John Bear, lead author of the book, is an expert on distance learning and the fallacy of diploma mills. His book will help you steer clear of any questionable institutions.

# Military Transcripts and Resources

Many colleges have designated military advisors on their staff to assist students in obtaining transcripts, financial aid, and other services. Since resources and policies are subject to change, students can contact representatives or advisors at the college where they are enrolled for the most current information.

You can also view the American Council on Education's *Guide to the Evaluation of Educational Experiences in the Armed Services* online at http://militaryguides.acenet.edu/index.htm, which contains recommendations for formal courses and occupations offered by the military services.

## Transcripts

In order to receive a credit evaluation for military service and training, request a transcript from the military branch using the links below. The transcripts will include training, experience, and standardized test scores. At your request, your official transcripts can be sent directly to the college or institution. Unofficial copies can also be sent to you. The transcripts are free of charge.

### Air Force

Community College of the Air Force (CCAF) @ http://www.au.af.mil/au/ccaf/transcripts.asp

### Army

Army/American Council on Education Registry Transcript System (AARTS) @ http://aarts.army.mil

Provides transcripts of military training and experience to Soldiers and Veterans of the Army, Army National Guard, and U.S. Army Reserve. Warrant or Commissioned Officers use the DD Form 295: Application for the Evaluation of Learning Experiences During Military Service.

## Coast Guard

U.S. Coast Guard Institute @ http://www.uscg.mil/hr/cgi

Type "transcript" into the site's search tool for links to information and request forms.

## Navy and Marine Corps

SMART Transcript @ https://smart.navy.mil/smart/welcome.do

# Additional Military Resources

Military.com @ http://www.military.com
For all branches of service. Click on the Education link at the top of the page.

GoArmyEd @ https://www.goarmyed.com

Servicemembers Opportunity Colleges @ http://www.soc.aascu.org

G.I. Bill and Educational Benefits Provided by the Department of Veterans Affairs @ http://www.gibill.va.gov

Yellow Ribbon Program for National Guard and Reserve Members @ http://www.yellowribbon.mil

# Sample Table of Contents for a Portfolio of Prior Learning

APPENDIX 5

Adult learner profile: Tim
Prior learning assessment portfolio

## Table of Contents

Section One: Introduction to PLA
    Goals Statements
    Signature of Authenticity
    Learning Chronology     2–10

Section Two: Prior Learning Narratives     11
    Managing Internet Information Systems/Web Design/E-mail     12–17
    Process Mapping and Process Improvement     18–22
    Business Communication     23–27
    Project Management     28–33
    Leadership     34–38
    References     39

Section Three: Supporting Documentation Index
    Document 1: HTML Code and Documents Created     40
    Document 2: Certificate of Completion HTML and HomeSite     41
    Document 3: Letter from Employer     42
    Document 4: Browser User Training Manual Excerpt     43
    Document 5: Status Report on Intranet     44
    Document 6: Process Mapping and Process
        Improvement (Various Documents)     45
    Document 7: Implementation Plans     46
    Document 8: System Documentation     47
    Document 9: Project Management—Certificate of Training     48

Document 10: Migration to Systems Memo      49
Document 11: Course Certificate      50
Document 12: Budget (numbers blacked out)      51
Document 13: Proposal      52
Document 14: Internal Memoranda (names blacked out)      53
Document 15: PowerPoint Training Handouts      54–55
Document 16: Performance Evaluation      56–59
Document 17: Transcripts      60

Appendix A: Petitions for Course Credit      61
Appendix B: Faculty Assessment Forms      62

# Course Research and Prewriting Strategy

Below is a course description Maria found online for an Introduction to Communication course.

## Introduction to Communication (3) COM 101 Lower Division

Provides an overview of communication and the competencies necessary to communicate effectively in today's society. Students will enhance their communication skills in interpersonal, small group, and public speaking settings.

## Key Terms and Concepts

From the course description, Maria had some idea of what the course covered, but she wanted more specific information on the topics. She found an Introduction to Communication textbook at her college library, which she used to identify key concepts within each of the topics listed in the course description. Based on her reading and analysis of the textbook, Maria created a basic outline for her narrative, as shown below.

Public speaking:

- Nonverbal and verbal elements
- Organization
- Visual aids
- Adapting to the audience

Interpersonal communication:

- Listening
- Perception
- Empathy
- Identity and culture
- Conflict resolution

Small groups:

- Roles and responsibilities
- Ground rules
- Facilitation
- Leadership styles

Here is an excerpt from Maria's portfolio showing her cover sheet, her statement of authenticity, and the portion of her narrative for the Intro to Communication course. Notice how she organized this section based on the outline she created using the course description and textbook (Appendix 6).

## Portfolio Cover Sheet and Statement of Authenticity

Portfolio for Prior Learning Assessment
*[Fill in name of college and office]*
Submitted to Community College
Adult Learning Assessment Office

Petition for requirements for the degree:
*[Degree or goal]*
Associate of Arts degree in Early Childhood Education
*[Current Month, Day, Year]*
September 20, 2009

Maria Rodriguez
*[Name]*
*[Student ID number]*
*[Address]*
*[Day and Evening Phone Numbers]*
*[Fax Number]*
*[E-mail Address]*

Signature and Statement of Authenticity
I, *[full name]*, certify that the information in this portfolio and the supporting documentation submitted is true, accurate, and represents my original work.

_____ (signature)    _____ (date)

# Narrative Format

## Introduction

In this prior learning portfolio, I will discuss my learning from being a wife and mother, in-home day care provider, employee at a domestic violence shelter, and assistant teacher at Head Start. I will also discuss how my experience as a Latina woman and educator has shaped my life. After writing my learning autobiography, I realized that I have learned more than my credentials will show. I have attended first aid and CPR courses from the American Montessori Society. I have attended training and a literacy conference through my Head Start program. However, what my credentials don't show is the lessons I've learned from many other life and work experiences. This narrative will demonstrate my learning.

In Spanish we have a saying that describes how I got along with my mother in my early adult years: it was "like water and oil" (which don't mix). Since maturing, I've appreciated how my mom pushed me and her other seven children to get an education. My goal is to obtain my associate's degree in early childhood education. And, that is just the beginning. When I graduate, I want to enter the combined bachelor's and master's degree program.

I will discuss in this narrative my learning related to the following subject areas: communication, cultural studies, early childhood teaching methods, first aid, and piano. The discussion that follows will be primarily about my learning in the first three subjects. The first aid learning will be documented with certificates and a brief explanation. The piano experience is documented with a videotape of me teaching children piano. In Section 3, I've included an index to my documents followed by the documents I'm using to support my petition for credit.

## Topic 1: Introduction to Communication

### Introduction to Communication (3) COM 101 Lower Division
Provides an overview of communication and the competencies necessary to communicate effectively in today's society. Students will enhance their communication skills in public speaking, interpersonal, and small group settings.

### Introduction

My mother insisted we speak and write English at home, so I grew up hearing Spanish and would defiantly respond to my mother and father's scolding in Spanish. Today, as a bilingual educator, communication is an essential part of my work. I have used communication skills in many settings, both at home and at work. When I was a day care provider, I had to communicate with parents about the needs of the children and the schedule. I used nonverbal communication with the babies and children to communicate a nurturing environment. When I worked in a domestic violence shelter, I had training on handling crisis calls and listening to clients during intakes. I even spoke in public with my knees knocking and my palms sweating. Now, I work in groups with 3-, 4-, and 5-year-old Latino children, teaching literacy and other skills. I continually learn at work and at home how to improve my skills. Communication is very important in building marriages and working on teams. Without my experience and mentors who helped me to improve my communication skills, I would have not pursued my dream to be an early childhood teacher. In this narrative, I will describe my experiential learning related to the following communication settings: public speaking, interpersonal communication, and small group communication.

## Public Speaking

Public speaking is hard, but once I did more and more, I got more confident. I could speak to a group of parents or a group of children, but speaking in front of a public audience was scary. I saw the PowerPoint presentations people made and they looked so professional. My supervisor at the shelter informed me that we received a grant that included education in the schools with teens, children, and parents. I had to pick up my nerve and do it. I was nervous about setting up audiovisual equipment, so I just started with simple visual aids and handouts. I knew that I talked too fast. So, when I was in a classroom I tried to remember to breathe and slow down to the pace of a creek, not a river. One time, I talked to second-graders about friendship and using words to handle disagreements. They looked at me so sweetly, that I smiled and relaxed. From then on, I started to like to speak with more confidence.

When I got better at organizing my ideas, I started with a fresh introduction, a body, and a conclusion that was geared to that audience's age. For young children, I discussed friendship, conflict resolution, and using words to talk about problems. We even did role-plays so the kids were involved. I talked about domestic violence myths to teens. I separated the girls because I noticed the boys would snicker and make rude remarks. I tried to be sensitive to the teacher's needs and preferences because I was presenting to a high school psychology class. The teacher told me that the teens liked the presentation I did, and there was good discussion. With adults, I allowed questions. Some of the questions surprised me because I didn't think the audience was always paying attention. I got better and better at involving audience participation and created a game, a poster, and scenarios. That way, I wasn't just doing all the talking. One time I prepared a hand-out with two spelling errors. After a teacher pointed it out, I was careful to review my materials. I gave at least 20 speeches one year and adapted it to all different ages and types of audiences.

Then, finally, it was time to try PowerPoint. It was easier to use than I thought. We had to meet with the grant committee and I wanted to be professional. I kept in mind the purpose: to inform the committee about how we used the funding we received and to persuade them about the need for future spending. I put the facts on slides and used graphics with two charts to show our numbers. I practiced so much and I was thinking about my speech all the time as if I was a president giving an address. I tried to consciously eliminate "um"s because I used them when I was nervous. I prepared an introduction with a statistic on the prevalence of domestic violence, so they would know why our program was important. I used seven slides, which was about right for the 10 minutes (see outline and slides in Document 3). I wanted to present the facts since they were looking for the numbers. I dressed professionally. I was glad that I learned to be calm. I talked to the panel and I looked at them respectfully. I received applause and questions. When I didn't know an answer to a question on statistics on the diversity of the populations we served, I said I'd get back to them, because I knew it was in the report but I didn't want to waste the panel's time thumbing through pages. I always told the truth. Later, I was told that we received re-funding, and I'm proud of that.

My experience in the Head Start classroom has helped me to project my voice without yelling. We use several classroom management techniques to get the children to look and listen. I also have to show assertiveness because especially when we are out on field trips or buses, I must have control of the children. When I lead music with the children, I always wait to get their attention first. I use my eyes when I'm playing the piano to look at the children who are off task. We use our bodies to communicate time and rhythm through clapping, stomping, and dance. I also have learned that transitions between activities have to be managed with music or a simple movement. I couldn't allow dead space. Nonverbal messages are very powerful.

Once I learned to manage my nervousness, I enjoyed giving speeches. It is hard to believe that this shy girl could speak in public. Over this year in my college classes, I had to give speeches as well. I noticed that some of the students just read their notes. At one time, I read my speeches. Now, I use note cards with key words on the organization of my speeches. I convinced my group on a group project in class to use PowerPoint with just the main ideas and some simple graphics. Our presentation was well received. Speaking is now one of my strengths. I am still getting better at using transitions from one of my points to another because I like to tell stories and can get off track. I remind myself to stay on the topic or I will confuse my audience. It also has helped to watch my teachers who are prepared and knowledgeable. I look forward to more public speaking experiences as a teacher.

## Supporting Documentation

Document 1—Letter from supervisor
Document 3—Statistics on the number of presentations
Document 4—Text of speech and PowerPoint miniatures
Document 8—Performance evaluation
Document 10—Transcript

## Interpersonal Communication

Interpersonal communication is a "dynamic process between or among people that touches people emotionally and psychologically" (Miller & Steinberg, 1975, p. 6). It is most associated with one-on-one communication. Interpersonal communication builds relationships or can tear them down. Interpersonal communication is different and more complex than "impersonal" communication. I use e-mail to get my work schedule and respond to simple messages, which are primarily simple "impersonal" messages. I use face-to-face interpersonal communication in my work with students, parents, and family members to build more meaningful relationships.

I learned about escalation and de-escalation of conflict during a difficult situation when a perpetrator found our shelter and stopped me when I was getting out of my car to start my shift. The man threatened to burn down the shelter unless I got his wife. I sat the man down first and I told him that I understood that he was angry. I could see that sitting him down made the situation less threatening and his volume decreased, so as not to arouse the clients in the home (the information on the clients is kept confidential). I asked him several open-ended questions about himself. At this time, the night manager saw the situation and pushed the emergency button. I was aware from her nonverbal messages that the police were on the way. Those 10 minutes felt like an eternity. However, the man opened up to me about his job loss and trying to keep up with insurance for one of his sick children. By the time the police arrived, the situation was de-escalated and the police also sat and talked with him for an hour. Finally, the man left peacefully.

I also learned that perception has a role in communication. I have seen that in my experiences. When I worked in the shelter, I had to see the perspective of the victims. It takes many times before a woman makes a decision to leave a violent relationship. Even though I had an opinion, I tried to understand the situation and listen empathically and repeat back (paraphrase) her feelings and anxieties.

Identity and culture impact communication. I noticed the reaction even in my day care to a child who wore braces on his legs. Sometimes his peers would not let them fit into their play; many times, he sat alone. It took months even after his braces were removed for the boy to mature socially, and I encouraged him every day to take more risks. Dealing with stressed-out parents was sometimes more difficult than taking care of the children. Once, there was a parent who was angry with me when her child made tortillas in my home because she thought my day care should have more educational activities. I found out later that she had difficulty with her cultural identity. Later, we became friends. I was glad that I was able to understand her perspective and move forward with our relationship. She also began to trust me and open up to me about her life.

Marriage is the most intimate of the one-on-one relationships. I've seen how raising children can become a priority and the relationship takes a back seat. My husband and I have taken our first vacation together ever after 20 years of marriage. I learned that you have to make relationships a priority or they can start to get stagnant. The priest at our parish recommended that we take time each week just to listen and get to know each other. This has helped us face changes in the empty nest phase of our lives.

Assertiveness is another skill I've used in conflict situations. If I don't say what's on my mind, I often act passively angry. Several of us read the book *Getting to Yes* by Fisher and Ury (1991) for an in-service training, which helped me see that there is often a win-win solution, but it takes both parties to share their needs. Often, we wind up with Lose-Lose or Lose-Win because we hide our interests and just stick to our position. In addition, I was able to attend training on mediation for children and adults given by the Mediation Project. During the mediation training, we were given a scenario and I had to play the neutral party to mediate and work through the steps of resolution. The first step was to let the parties vent. Then, they could work through the solution process. In many schools, children are trained to be mediators for conflicts. It was amazing to watch a video of elementary school children who were trained as mediators.

At Head Start, I realized that when talking to a two-year-old, I need to bend down, get at their level, and speak at their level. I learned how babies need touch in order to thrive. Nonverbal and verbal messages interrelate—support, add, help, and emphasize ideas. We use nonverbal messages to help the child with literacy by pronouncing words with emphasis, using exaggerated facial expressions and even music and dance. It's amazing to watch how their communication skills improve with their social and intellectual development.

Communication is a complex process where the need to adapt to the situation is very important. It sometimes is interrupted by noise, which can be as simple as a noisy classroom or as complex as the thoughts in our heads. This is also referred to as intrapersonal communication or communication with yourself. I noticed that even giving myself positive messages impacted the way I related to others. Interpersonal skills are ones that I can constantly learn and improve upon.

## Supporting Documentation

Document 1—Letter from supervisor
Document 2—Certificate of training—Mediation Project
Document 7—Annotated bibliography
Document 8—Performance evaluation
Document 9—Letter from day care parent
Document 11—Certificate of training—intake skills

## Small Group Communication

At Head Start we work with the children in groups. Even in the five-year-old groups, leaders emerge and the children take on different roles. We use a child-centered approach and we integrate children with disabilities in our groups with children who do not have disabilities. Our group work is designed to enhance the cognitive and social development of the children and their families. As a group leader, I have to be sensitive to time and task (we have 130 children in our school and share resources and classrooms). I also have to be aware of group dynamics: for example, where two children sit next to each other may impact their concentration. I noticed that the kids knew when I wasn't listening or was just faking it, and they acted out. It takes hard work and concentration to be attentive to the group.

Also, I worked with groups of adults at the shelter (I was not the therapist but the assistant). Just from observing great communicators such as the group therapist, I was able to make adjustments in my skills. I noticed how they used group rules or norms, for instance, that a person did not have to talk. Then, the group leader reminded the group of the rule that they had agreed upon (see Document 6). When I contributed, I tried never to interrupt, but I noticed there was usually a dominant person. When that occurred, we tried to make comments such as "Let's hear from someone else." I've observed that turn-taking can be difficult for both children and adults. I also became aware of the role of the summarizer. Sometimes, this role was very important to bring across the points already covered.

In the Head Start workplace I could observe different types of leadership styles. Some of the bosses were more rigid (authoritarian) about how things were run and the decisions to set schedules and policies. Others used a more democratic style and heard everyone's voice on problems and scheduling. Even though this style took more work, I saw the results were better. I saw the laissez-faire leadership style in one teacher who sort of let the group do what they wanted. This person did not last long in our team environment. Also, we were able to attend a conference on literacy and I heard talks from visionary leaders in the Latino community who were setting the direction for the future of education. I was able to witness leadership styles that motivated me to continue my education.

### Supporting Documentation

Document 1—Letter from supervisor
Document 5—Conference brochure—"Vision for the Future of Biliteracy Instruction"
Document 6—Group rules
Document 8—Performance evaluation

## Conclusion

A supportive, open climate and adaptability are important in communication. Effective communication takes time, effort, and concentration to overcome the barriers. My communication skills have improved because I use them on a daily basis and have observed other mentors with excellent classroom management and facilitation skills. I hope to use and improve upon my skills in the classroom, at home, and with my coworkers by listening to the feedback from my supervisors and obtaining even more training in my profession.

# Sample Three-Part Competency Statement

Depending on the college's requirements, Maria could use a three-part format to describe her learning like the one below.

| DESCRIPTION OF EXPERIENCE | LEARNING FROM EXPERIENCE | DOCUMENTATION |
|---|---|---|
| | Topic 1: Public Speaking | |
| Prepared and presented 20 presentations on domestic violence and prevention to children, teens, and parents for La Familia during a two-and-a-half-year time period. | Adapted effectively to the age and experience of the audience. | 1—Letter from supervisor |
| | Organized a presentation into an introduction, body, and conclusion. | 3—Statistics on presentations |
| | Prepared appropriate handouts and visual aids for the audiences that were attractive, accurate, and free of errors. | |
| | Paid careful attention to delivery aspects such as eye contact, volume, pauses, facial expressions, tone, rate, and body language. | 8—Performance evaluations |
| | Prepared and rehearsed so that the transitions between points sounded natural. | |
| | Managed nervousness to appear confident and composed. | |
| | Eliminated filler words such as "um" by pausing silently. | |

(continued)

| DESCRIPTION OF EXPERIENCE | LEARNING FROM EXPERIENCE | DOCUMENTATION |
|---|---|---|
| Prepared and delivered a formal PowerPoint presentation to a grant committee (La Familia). | Read the requirements and organized the speech to meet the requirements.<br><br>Paid careful attention to purpose (information and persuasion) and needs of audience (result-oriented, time-stressed, and focused).<br><br>Used PowerPoint effectively by not filling the slides with too much written text and building one idea per slide.<br><br>Found current and reliable sources for statistics to persuade the audience of the need to re-fund the project.<br><br>Timed the speech to meet the limits.<br><br>Answered questions truthfully. | 4—Speech and PowerPoint slides |
| Led three-, four- and five-year-old children for two years in lesson plans, music classes, and activities (Head Start). | Used classroom management techniques consistently.<br><br>Used exaggerated gestures and nonverbal communication to maintain the children's interest.<br><br>Spoke clearly to help children with literacy.<br><br>Used an appropriate level of vocabulary. | 1—Letter from supervisor |
| Worked with a group on formal classroom presentations. | Designed visual aids and handouts to reflect all of the speaker's key ideas.<br><br>Used a consistent format.<br><br>Practiced presentation with the entire group to get feedback. | 4—Speech and PowerPoint slides<br><br><br><br>10—Transcript |

(continued)

| DESCRIPTION OF EXPERIENCE | LEARNING FROM EXPERIENCE | DOCUMENTATION |
|---|---|---|
| Topic 2: Interpersonal Communication | | |
| Worked with children at Head Start. | Understood, observed, and appreciated the Latino culture. | 8—Performance evaluations |
| | Used nonverbal messages to interact with young children. | |
| Worked in a domestic violence shelter two-and-a-half years doing intakes and educational outreach (La Familia). | Respected the confidentiality of all clients. | 1—Letter from supervisor |
| | Understood how a woman's desire to leave may be misperceived. | |
| | Used de-escalation (sitting, talking quietly) with a conflict with an angry perpetrator until the police arrived. | |
| | Read and applied *Getting to Yes* (Fisher and Ury, 1991). | 7—Annotated bibliography |
| | Attended and applied mediation training from the Mediation Project. | 2—Certificate of training—Mediation Project |
| | Taught school children a step-by-step conflict resolution process. | |
| | Appreciated the complexity of human communication. | |
| Managed a licensed day care in my home for seven years. | Worked effectively with parents to hear their concerns. | 9—Letter from day care mom |
| | Began a strong friendship with a parent from my day care when she disclosed the root of biases as a Latina woman. | |
| | Learned to withhold first impressions and judgments in order to listen more effectively. | |
| | Worked with a disabled boy to help him mature socially. | |
| | Appreciated that touch could help a baby thrive. | |

(continued)

| DESCRIPTION OF EXPERIENCE | LEARNING FROM EXPERIENCE | DOCUMENTATION |
|---|---|---|
| Married for 20 years. Raised (with my husband) two sons. | Learned to take more time for dates with my husband.<br><br>Taught my sons respect for all races and for women. | |

Topic 3: Small Group Communication

| DESCRIPTION OF EXPERIENCE | LEARNING FROM EXPERIENCE | DOCUMENTATION |
|---|---|---|
| Led small groups in Head Start classrooms and interacted with staff. | Learned a child-centered approach and methods to integrate children with disabilities. | 1—Letter from supervisor |
| | Observed different leadership styles (authoritarian, laissez-faire) and how the democratic supervisors allowed everyone's concerns to be heard. | 8—Performance evaluations |
| | Practiced asking and answering questions without defensiveness. | |
| | Attended a conference and witnessed visionary leadership. | 5—Conference brochure |
| | Appreciated how a leader could affect the climate of the whole organization. | |
| Led discussions with groups of teens.<br><br>Assisted therapists in groups at La Familia. | Divided the teen girls from the boys during the discussion period in order to get better responses. | 8—Performance evaluations |
| | Learned and applied group rules. | 6—Group rules |
| | Learned to handle group members who monopolized discussions | |
| | Appreciated the role of a facilitator to help bring members to a new awareness. | |
| | Observed and practiced the role of summarizer. | |

# Sample Letter of Verification

(Letterhead used)

Dear Portfolio Evaluator,

This letter testifies that Maria Rodriguez was employed at La Familia on a part-time basis during the period of Nov. 2000 to May 2002. I was the coordinator of the grant program and the domestic violence shelter and hired Maria. Maria worked in our shelter and assisted with educational grant-funded domestic violence prevention programs in the office, in schools, and in the community.

During her employment, Maria used strong communication skills in numerous settings. She interacted effectively with our clients on the telephone, in person, and in classrooms. Maria used mature judgment in respecting the confidentiality of our clients and listening to their needs in order to accurately reflect the client's situation on our intake forms. I think one of her strengths was her ability to ask questions and to listen empathically to the answers. Many of our clients came in crisis situations and Maria helped them make the transition. Maria was called on numerous times to provide translation for our Spanish-speaking clients. She adapted well to stressful situations. Maria gave a presentation to our grant committee, which was well received. Maria also learned to overcome her shyness in public speaking by providing training in the classroom to children and parents. She was able to adapt her language and visual aids to both groups effectively. Maria's dedication to raising her children gave her the ability to relate well to other parents and children at the shelter. On her performance evaluation, Maria's communication skills were ranked high (4.5 out of possible 5).

I wish Maria all the best in her educational endeavors. Please feel free to contact me for more information.

Sincerely,

Name of supervisor, title, address, e-mail address, phone number

# Sample Faculty Evaluation

As you know by now, methods of submission and assessment vary from college to college. For instance:

- Is the portfolio submitted as one petition for all subject areas or separate submissions for each subject area?
- Do individual faculty members evaluate the portfolio or is there a panel of evaluators?
- Are there specific criteria for credit based on outcomes or general criteria based on college level learning or competencies?
- Is the portfolio given a grade of credit/no credit (most common) or a letter grade?

### Excerpt from faculty evaluation of Maria's portfolio:

Generally, the committee found that Maria's portfolio was well organized and well documented. The learning chronology set the context for her learning. The writing was at college level but had several grammatical errors. The petitioner requested credits that are aligned with her goal of associate degree in early childhood education. The committee assigns credit for learning that is the equivalent of a 70% or C minus level or higher.

The competencies for first aid and piano were strong and complete, and the supporting documentation was sufficient for the awards. The only learning gap identified in the first aid petition was the recognition for continuing education as the first aid and CPR standards are updated. The student showed above the competency levels for introductory learning in music theory and applications for special needs children. The inclusion of dance and song techniques used by the petitioner impressed the panel. The methods petition showed experience in the classroom and understanding of literacy but lacked a broader understanding of education principles. Maria will benefit from her coursework in educational theories and principles of multiculturalism. The petition for Comparing Cultures demonstrated mature awareness, but was awarded two credits due to the minimal experiential learning of cultures outside the Latino culture. The demonstration of learning in Introduction to Communication was enhanced by the other petitions including the discussion of culture and educational methods. The documentation, especially the text of the speech Maria presented before the grant committee, demonstrated above-average speech-preparation skills. The petitioner's experience was adequately verified with letters from two supervisors.

See notes in the portfolio from faculty subject matter experts on the rationale for the assessment.

The faculty assessing committee awards the following:

Petition for 14 credits (based on quarter hours.) Awarded 11 credits in the following areas *[no grades assigned because this college's awards are credit/no credit]*

Early Childhood Education Methods (2)—Average rating

Comparing Cultures (2)—Average rating

Introduction to Communication (3)—Average rating with above average in public speaking

First Aid (1)—Above average rating

Piano Class I (3)—Above average rating

A copy of this record will be sent to the records office for transcription.

The student has 30 days to appeal this decision to the chair of the assessment committee. Appeals policies are located at the assessment office.

# Glossary of Terms

**AACRAO**—The American Association of Collegiate Registrars and Admissions Officers whose mission is "to serve and advance higher education by providing leadership in academic and enrollment services" (http://www.aacrao.org).

**academic advisor**—A person employed by the college (often a faculty member) who assists students with degree planning and prior learning assessment options.

**academic year**—The time period of academic instruction, which is divided into semesters, quarters, or trimesters.

**accreditation**—Recognition of a college by an independent private organization. Accreditation is a factor in the transfer of credits from institution to institution. There are six regional accrediting bodies as well as nearly one hundred national, professional, and specialized accrediting bodies recognized by the U.S. Secretary of Education or the Council for Higher Education Accreditation (CHEA).

**accreditation mill**—An entity that unethically awards accreditations to colleges that do not meet widely accepted standards.

**accredited institutions**—Colleges and universities that have acquired accreditation of their programs.

**ACE**—American Council on Education. ACE "provides leadership on key higher education issues and influences public policy through advocacy, research, and program initiatives" (http://www.acenet.edu).

**ACT**—American College Testing program, which administers aptitude and achievement tests including the ACT college entrance exam (http://www.act.org).

**admissions**—The application process for entry and the decision to admit a prospective student into a college. For students, the admissions process may include completing an application, requesting transcripts, or taking competency exams.

**adult-friendly colleges**—A term describing colleges that intentionally provide services for the adult learner.

**adult learner**—In most institutions, a student over the age of 24 who often attends college part time, is financially independent from parents, has a job outside of school, and delays enrollment in postsecondary education beyond the first year after high school graduation (from *Adult Learners in Higher Education,* 2007); as distinguished from the "traditional" student who is 18 to 24 years old and enters college immediately after high school.

**articulation**—The system used by colleges to recognize course equivalency.

**articulation agreement**—Agreements among colleges or programs regarding the transfer of credit. For example, a four-year college may have an articulation agreement with a two-year college to seamlessly transfer a student's credit.

**artifacts**—Also known as "documentation" or "exhibits," these are items that demonstrate or verify a student's learning.

**assessment**—The process of evaluating a student's learning; when referring to prior learning assessment (PLA), the process through which college-level credit is awarded or denied.

**assessment fee**—The cost of assessment of a student's learning for college-level credit. Fees vary from institution to institution and may be one lump sum or charged per credit awarded.

**assessor**—Also known as a faculty evaluator, this is a faculty member or expert in the subject area being assessed who is responsible for evaluating a prior learning candidate's portfolio.

**associate's degree**—A degree awarded to a student who completes the equivalent of two years of full-time coursework (typically 60–64 semester hours or 105–120 quarter hours in the U.S.).

**bachelor's degree**—A degree awarded to a student who completes the equivalent of four years of full-time coursework (typically 120–128 semester hours in the U.S.). In other countries the bachelor's degree generally takes three years.

**Bloom's Taxonomy**—A learning theory developed by a committee led by Benjamin Bloom that describes three domains of educational activities: cognitive, affective, and psychomotor (knowledge, attitude, and skills).

**CAEL**—The Council for Adult and Experiential Learning (http:// www.cael. org) links learning and work. CAEL works at all levels within the higher education, public, and private sectors to make it easier for people to get the education and training they need. CAEL publishes the standards for the assessment of learning that colleges use to create policies and procedures for their prior learning assessment programs.

**case study**—A tool the assessor can use that allows a learner to demonstrate his or her learning as it applies to a specific situation.

**certificate**—A document stating that a student has gained competency or proficiency in a subject matter as well as listing where the competency was achieved. A certificate can be awarded for completion, such as completing one computer software course. Some colleges administer certificate programs after a student passes a required number of credits (such as 20 credit hours in telecommunications or 15 credits in human resources). Depending on the college, the credits earned may be eligible for transfer toward a degree program.

**CEU**—Typically given in training courses, a Continuing Education Unit is often awarded for educational experiences that help meet the designation of a professional organization such as a teacher or a lab technician. The International Association for Continuing Education and Training defines one CEU as the equivalent of "ten contact hours of participation in an organized CE/T experience, delivered under responsible sponsorship, capable direction and qualified instruction." CEUs alone are rarely considered the equivalent of academic credit.

**challenge exam**—An examination written by instructors at their respective colleges that is given to learners to assess whether their learning equates to a college course. The challenge exam may be similar in content to the final exam given in a course.

**CHEA**—The Council for Higher Education Accreditation promotes "academic quality through formal recognition of higher education accrediting bodies" (http://www.chea.org).

**CLEP**—The College-Level Examination Program, a national program that provides standardized examinations in a number of subject matters allowing students to earn college credit for their learning (http:// clep.collegeboard.org).

**college**—In the U.S., an institution offering programs leading to the associate (two-year) degree, bachelor's (four-year) degree, or a higher degree. Or, a specific college in a university may refer to a part of an institution or field within the university (e.g., Daniels Business College at the University of Denver).

**College Board**—An education advocacy group and the publishers of CLEP exams (http://www.collegeboard.org).

**college level**—A determination made by faculty, colleges, and accrediting bodies. Course competencies, course descriptions, and course syllabi assist in recognizing the type, depth, and breadth of learning that is considered college level.

**community college**—A school offering programs leading to the associate degree. May also offer non-credit courses and labs on such topics as writing, English as a second language, or math. Also called a junior college.

**competencies or competency**—When referring to prior learning assessment, competencies are used in awarding credit or degrees based on learning outcomes rather than on time spent.

**contexts**—Circumstances surrounding a place or time. In prior learning assessment, one measure of a candidate's learning is whether the learning is applicable or transferable to other contexts.

**continuing education**—Courses offered in a number of venues, such as schools or community education centers, that are targeted to adults. In some cases, the courses may be offered for college credit.

**course**—A specific unit of instruction, such as a course in microeconomics or abnormal psychology.

**course challenge**—See challenge exam.

**credit**—A unit used to record and measure a formal course, typically based on the number of hours spent on coursework each week.

**critical incidents**—Events that result in changed thinking, attitudes, or actions.

**curriculum**—A program of courses or subjects taken in pursuit of a degree or other objective.

**DANTES**—The Defense Activity for Non-Traditional Education Support, a body that provides a variety of educational opportunities, regulates financial aid programs, and administers equivalency exams for active military (http://www.dantes.doded.mil).

**degree**—An academic title given by a school to show that a certain course of study has been completed (e.g., associate degree, bachelor's degree).

**degree plan**—A detailed description of the program and courses an applicant or enrolled student plans to pursue. The process of mapping out coursework to complete a degree is also known as academic, degree, or coursework planning.

**DETC**—Distance Education and Training, a type of accreditation given to colleges that differs from regional accreditation.

**digitize**—When you digitize something, you convert it to a digital format. For example, students digitize supporting documents before uploading them to an electronic portfolio by using a scanner to digitize paper or a digital camera to digitize images.

**diploma**—The certificate that shows a certain type of study has been completed. Diplomas are awarded for completing a degree or course of study.

**diploma mill**—An unethical, unaccredited institution that issues a worthless degree for a fee.

**discipline**—A field of study, such as business, or computer science.

**distance learning**—Also known as online learning, distance education, or distributed learning, this type of learning relies on educational technologies such as the Internet, CDs, or video for delivery.

**documentation**—Articles used to support or verify a petition for credit for prior learning experience. May include certificates, artifacts, letters, licenses, or training records

**DSST**—Formerly known simply as DANTES or the DANTES Subject Standardized Tests. DSST is another national program (like CLEP) that provides examinations in a number of subjects allowing students to earn college credit for their prior learning (http://www.getcollegecredit.com).

**electives**—Also known as general electives, open electives, or free electives, these are courses taken to fulfill degree requirements that are not requirements for the major or core studies, but selected to fill a degree program.

**electronic portfolio**—A compilation of work samples, certificates, verification letters, etc., hosted on the Web with programs that interface with a database, allowing the archived contents to be uploaded and viewed online. Also known as e-portfolios, Webfolios, or digital portfolios, they are commonly used to build career portfolios, demonstrate writing, or show competencies in teacher education programs.

**experiential learning**—Direct learning or learning through work, hands-on experience, or community service.

**faculty**—College instructors employed at a university. Also known as lecturers, facilitators, adjunct faculty members, or professors.

**fees**—Money paid to a school for purposes other than tuition. Fees for assessment services are paid upfront. In accordance with CAEL standards, fees for assessment services are paid for the service performed, not for the number of credits awarded.

**financial aid**—Scholarships, loans, fellowships, tuition reductions, or other methods of financial payment to the college. Many schools have a financial aid department to manage financial aid questions.

**full-time student**—Normally considered a student who is enrolled in 12 semester hours or more of credit in a given term.

**GED**—General Educational Development tests measure a student's knowledge and academic skills. The GED is considered the equivalent of a traditional high school degree.

**goals statement**—A possible component of a portfolio, it is designed to help PLA candidates clarify short- and long-term personal, educational, or career goals.

**grade point average**—The average score a student has made in all of his or her classes, weighted by the number of credits or units for each class. Also called GPA.

**graduate**—A person who has earned a degree from a school. In the U.S. graduate programs are offered beyond the bachelor's (also known as postgraduate) degree.

**Kolb's model of experiential learning**—David Kolb's four-stage theory of learning from experience illustrates how experiential learning is a cycle involving concrete experience, reflection and observation, abstract conceptualization, and active experimentation.

**learning**—Knowledge, skills, and abilities gained through experience.

**learning narrative**—An essay with personal reflections, stories, and insights specific to the course outcomes being petitioned.

**major**—The subject or academic department in which a student takes his or her concentrations (such as a computer science major).

**metacognitive process**—"Knowing about knowing"; learners' awareness of their own knowledge, especially about when and how to use certain strategies for learning or problem solving.

**mind mapping**—A creative way of organizing thoughts and ideas visually by using diagrams or graphics linked to and arranged around a central idea or key word.

**minor**—The secondary subject or academic department outside the major in which a student takes concentrated coursework (generally, four or more courses in an area of study).

**multiple intelligences**—Categories that describe people's preferred learning styles, behavioral and working styles, and natural strengths. In addition to the basic seven intelligences (logical-mathematical, linguistic, spatial, musical, body-kinesthetic, interpersonal, and intrapersonal), Howard Gardner has added naturalist, spiritual/existential, and moral.

**narrative**—An essay with personal reflections, stories [anecdotes], and insights.

**part-time student**—Normally, a student who is enrolled in fewer than 12 hours of credit per term.

**petition**—To request or ask for.  A student prepares a portfolio requesting 30 credit hours; the faculty members review the material for "college-level" learning and may conclude that all credit hours can be awarded or only a portion of the credits.

**portfolio**—A formal communication presented by a student to the college as part of a petition requesting credit or recognition for learning outside the college classroom. The portfolio must make its case by identifying learning clearly and succinctly, and it must provide sufficient supporting information and documentation so that faculty can use it, alone or in combination with other evidence, as the basis for their evaluations (Lamdin, 1992, p. 84). The portfolio is the package used in assigning academic credit for learning

**prerequisites**—Courses that must be completed first before enrolling in more advanced coursework.

**prior learning assessment (PLA)**—A term used by colleges and universities to describe the process of earning college credit from learning acquired through a student's work, training, volunteer experiences, and personal life. Also known as assessment of prior learning (APL), prior learning assessment and recognition (PLAR), and flexible assessment (a term used in the UK.).

**registrar**—The office or department at colleges that maintains official student records such as academic records and transcripts.

**résumé**—A summary of work experience including dates, sources, and description of work. A résumé used in a prior learning assessment portfolio may include volunteer work, hobbies, or training.

**semester hour**—An amount of credit earned in a course, normally representing one hour of course instruction per week for a semester.

**supporting documentation**—See **documentation**.

**syllabus**—A detailed outline of a course written by a faculty member that may include course goals, textbooks, instructor contact information, learning outcomes, schedules, policies, course topics, evaluation, and grading criteria.

**tacit knowledge**—"Personal knowledge embedded in individual experience and involving intangible factors, such as personal beliefs, perspectives, and value systems. Hard to articulate with formal language, tacit knowledge contains subjective insights, intuitions, and hunches" (Clark, 2010). An often untapped source of knowledge that, when used by learners, adds an exciting richness to the learning.

**threaded discussion**—A chronological list of online comments and discussion points on a topic. Threaded discussions differ from chat rooms, which facilitate online discussions in real time, similar to instant messaging.

**TOEFL**—The Test of English as a Foreign Language (http://www.ets.org/toefl), which measures English language proficiency.

**transcript**—An official document that lists courses taken by a student, grades received, and credit awarded (degree awarded). Official transcripts have the imprint of the school's seal. Unofficial transcripts are copies without the official seal.

**transfer student**—A student who has earned credit in one school and then applies the credit to another school's program.

**transformational learning**—Life-altering insights that change one's perception of self and the world.

**tuition**—The amount a college charges for courses (U.S. term only).

**tuition benefits**—A workplace benefit in which the employer pays all or part of an employee's cost to attend college or university classes. Most tuition assistance programs require the employee to earn a passing grade of "C" or better to receive the benefit.

**undergraduate**—Period of study leading up to the awarding of the associate's or bachelor's degree.

**university**—An educational institution that includes graduate and professional schools awarding master's degrees and doctorates in addition to an undergraduate division that awards bachelor's degrees. Many universities offer adult-oriented or adult-friendly programs.

# References

## Chapter 1

American Council on Education. (2005). *Find an ACE-reviewed training course provider*. Retrieved August 30, 2005, from http://www.acenet.edu/AM/Template.cfm?Section=Organizational_Services&Template=/CM/HTMLDisplay.cfm&ContentID=6034

Bahr, M. (2002, October). From job security to career mobility: The importance of lifelong learning. *Centerpoint*. Retrieved September 7, 2004, from http://www.acenet.edu/clll/centerpoint/index.cfm?articleID=114

Brigham, C., & Klein-Collin, R. (2010). *Availability, use, and value of prior learning assessment within community colleges.* Chicago, IL: CAEL.

Bureau of Labor Statistics. (2004). *Occupational outlook handbook, 2004–05 edition*. Washington, DC: U.S. Department of Labor. Retrieved August 30, 2005, from http://www.bls.gov/oco/

Bureau of Labor Statistics. (2011, May 4). *Education pays in higher earning and lower unemployment rates.* Washington, DC: U.S. Department of Labor. Retrieved from http://www.bls.gov/emp/ep_chart_001.htm

CAEL. (n.d.). *Report to the National Commission on Accountability in Higher Education*. Retrieved August 30, 2005, from http://www.sheeo.org/account/comm/testim/CAEL%20testimony.pdf

CAEL. (2010, March). *Fueling the race to postsecondary success: A 48-institution study of prior learning assessment and adult student outcomes.* Chicago, IL: Author.

Carnevale, A. P., Smith, N., & Strohl, J. (2010, June). *Help wanted: Projections of jobs and education requirements through 2018.* Washington, DC: Georgetown University Center on Education and the Workforce. Retrieved from http://www9.georgetown.edu/grad/gppi/hpi/cew/pdfs/FullReport.pdf

College Board. (2010a). *Trends in college pricing 2010*. Retrieved from http://trends.collegeboard.org/downloads/College_Pricing_2010.pdf

College Board. (2010b). *Trends in student aid 2010*. Retrieved from http://trends.collegeboard.org/downloads/Student_Aid_2010.pdf

College Board. (2011a). *About CLEP*. Retrieved July 15, 2011, from http://www.collegeboard.com/student/testing/clep/about.html

College Board. (2011b). *Colleges granting CLEP tests.* Retrieved July 15, 2011, from http://apps.collegeboard.com/cbsearch_clep/searchCLEPColleges.jsp

Day, J. C., & Newburger, E. C. (2002, July). *The big payoff: Educational attainment and synthetic estimates of work-life earnings.* Washington, DC: U.S. Department of Commerce, Economics and Statistics Administration, U.S. Census Bureau. Retrieved August 30, 2005, from http://www.census.gov/prod/2002pubs/p23-210.pdf

Dow, G. (2004). Assessment of prior learning (APL). *Community College of Vermont.* Quote used with permission. Retrieved September 7, 2004, from http://www.ccv.edu/APL

Hart, D., & Hickerson, J. (2009). *Prior learning portfolios: A representative collection.* Dubuque, IA: Kendall Hunt.

Kolb, D. A. (1984). *Experiential learning.* Englewood Cliffs, NJ: Prentice Hall.

Lamdin, L. (1992). *Earn college credit for what you know.* Chicago, IL: CAEL.

LeGrow, M., Sheckley, B., & Kehrhahn, M. (Fall 2002). Comparison of problem-solving performance between adults receiving credit via assessment of prior learning and adults completing classroom courses. *The Journal of Continuing Higher Education, 50*(3), 2–13.

Lumina Foundation. (2005). *Adult learners.* Retrieved October 17, 2005, from http://www.luminafoundation.org/adult_learners/

University Professional and Continuing Education Association. (2010). *Frequently asked questions: How is the non-traditional student defined?* Retrieved July 28, 2011, from http://upcea.edu/resources/faqs.html

Voorhees, R., & Lingenfelter, P. (2003). *Adult learners and state policy.* Retrieved August 30, 2005, from http://www.sheeo.org/workfrce/CAEL%20paper.pdf

Whitaker, U. (1989). *Assessing learning: Standards, principles, and procedures.* Chicago, IL: CAEL.

Zuckerman, M. B. (2004, March 8). A truly cruel college squeeze. *U.S. News and World Report, 136*(8), 80.

## Chapter 2

ACE. (2003, August). Student success: Understanding graduation and persistence rates. *ACE Issue Brief.* Retrieved September 20, 2004, from http://www.acenet.edu/programs/policy

Allen, I. E., & Seaman, J. (2010). *Class differences: Online education in the United States, 2010.* Babson Park, MA: Babson Survey Research Group.

Bolles, R. N. (2011). *What color is your parachute? A practical manual for job-hunters and career-changers.* Berkeley, CA: Ten Speed Press.

Collins, J. (2001). *Good to great.* New York, NY: Harper Business Books.

Gross, R. (1999). *Peak learning.* New York, NY: Putman.

Ibarra, H. (2003). *Working identity: Unconventional strategies for reinventing your career.* Boston, MA: Harvard Business School Press.

Wlodkowski, R. J. (1998). *Enhancing adult motivation to learn: A comprehensive guide for teaching all adults.* San Francisco, CA: Jossey-Bass.

Zizzi, M. P. (2003). *Successful communication for adult learners.* Retrieved from http://academic.regis.edu/ed205/additional_articles.html

## Chapter 4

Fiddler, M., Marienau, C., & Whitaker, U. (2006). *Assessing learning: Standards, principles, and procedures*. (2nd ed.). Dubuque, IA: Kendall Hunt.

Office of Institutional Research and Assessment, University of Wisconsin-Green Bay. (n.d.). *Credit for prior learning: Words of wisdom from faculty reviewers*. Used with permission. Retrieved August 20, 2004, from http://www.uwgb.edu/oira/cfpl/portfolio/wisdom.asp

Whitaker, U. (1989). *Assessing learning: Standards, principles, and procedures*. Chicago, IL: CAEL.

## Chapter 5

ACE. (2005). *Find an ACE-reviewed training course provider.* Retrieved September 1, 2005, from http://www.acenet.edu/AM/Template.cfm?Section=Organizational_Services&Template=/CM/HTMLDisplay.cfm&ContentID=6034

Council for Higher Education Accreditation. (2011). *Important questions about accreditation, diploma mills, and accreditation mills.* Retrieved July 20, 2011, from http://www.chea.org/degreemills/

## Chapter 6

Gross, R. (1999). *Peak learning: How to create your own lifelong education program for personal enlightenment and professional success*. New York, NY: Putman.

Koch, R. (1998). *The 80/20 principle: The secret of achieving more with less*. New York, NY: Currency.

## Chapter 7

Arnold, S., Warner, W. J., & Osborne, E. W. (2006). Experiential learning in secondary agricultural education classrooms. *Journal of Southern Agricultural Education Research, 56*(1), 30–39. Retrieved August 12, 2011, from http://www.jsaer.org/pdf/Vol56/56-01-030.pdf

Boud, D., Keogh, R., & Walker, D. (1985). What is reflection in learning? In D. Boud, R. Keogh, & D. Walker (Eds.), *Reflection: Turning experience into learning* (pp. 7–17). London: Croom Helm.

Bloom, B., & Krathwohl, D. (1956). *Taxonomy of educational objectives: The classification of educational goals. Handbook I: Cognitive Domain*. New York, NY: Longmans, Green.

Brookfield, S. (1990). Using critical incidents to explore learners' assumptions. In Mezirow, J. (Ed.), *Fostering critical reflection in adulthood: A guide to transformative and emancipatory learning* (pp. 177–193). San Francisco, CA: Jossey-Bass.

Brookfield, S. (2006). *Developing critical thinkers.* Retrieved August 15, 2011, from http://www.stephenbrookfield.com/Dr._Stephen_D._Brookfield/Workshop_Materials_files/Critical_Thinking_materials.pdf

Coleman, J. S. (1976). Differences between experiential and classroom learning. In M. Keeton et al. (Eds.), *Experiential learning: Rationale, characteristics, and assessment* (pp. 49–61). San Francisco, CA: Jossey-Bass.

Cooper, D. (1998). *Reading, writing, and reflection*. San Francisco, CA: Jossey-Bass.

Fiddler, M., Marienau, C., & Whitaker, U. (2006). *Assessing learning: Standards, principles, and procedures* (2nd ed.). Dubuque, IA: Kendall Hunt.

Foley, G. (2004). *Dimensions of adult learning*. Berkshire, GBR: McGraw-Hill Education.

Gardner, H. (1983). *Frames of mind*. New York, NY: Basic Books.

Gardner, H. (2000). *Intelligence reframed: Multiple intelligences for the 21st century*. New York, NY: Basic Books.

Goleman, D. (2006). *Emotional intelligence: Why it can matter more than IQ* (10th ed.). New York, NY: Bantam Books.

Kikoski, C. K., & Kikoski, J. F. (2004). *The inquiring organization: Tacit knowledge, conversation, and knowledge creation: Skills for 21st-century organizations*. Westport, CT: Praeger.

Kolb, D. (1984). *Experiential learning: Experience as the source of learning and development*. Englewood Cliffs, NJ: Prentice Hall.

Knowles, M. S. (1975). *Self-directed learning*. New York, NY: Cambridge Books.

Knowles, M. S. (1984). *The adult learner: A neglected species* (3rd ed.). Houston, TX: Gulf Publishing.

Luckner, J. L., & Nadler, R. S. (1997). *Processing the experience: Strategies to enhance and generalize learning*. Dubuque, IA: Kendall Hunt.

Passarelli, A. M., & Kolb, D. A. (2011). The learning way—Learning from experience as the path to lifelong learning and development. In M. London.\ (Ed.), *The Oxford handbook of lifelong learning*. New York, NY: Oxford University Press USA.

Raelin, J. A. (2008). *Work-based learning: Bridging knowledge and action in the workplace*. San Francisco, CA: Jossey-Bass.

Rylatt, A. (2003). *Winning the knowledge game: Smarter learning for business excellence*. Oxford: Butterworth-Heinemann.

Schöen, D. A. (1987). *Educating the reflective practitioner: Toward a new design for teaching and learning in the professions* (1st ed.). San Francisco, CA: Jossey-Bass.

Whitaker, U. (1989). *Assessing learning: Standards, principles, and procedures*. Chicago, IL: CAEL.

## Chapter 8

Durkin, T. (1998, July). *PLA in search of the diploma.* Speech given at the 1998 PLA conference in Canada. Retrieved November 15, 2004, from http://www.tyendinaga.net/fnti/prior/plafn_tl.htm

## Chapter 9

Younger, D., Colvin, J., Dewees, P., Graybill, M., & Michelson, A. (2005). *Prior learning assessment workshop manual*. Chicago, IL: CAEL.

## Chapter 11

Alliance for Telecommunications Industry Solutions. (2011). *ATIS telecom glossary*. Retrieved July 26, 2011, from http://www.atis.org/glossary/

Batson, T. (2002, December 1). *The electronic portfolio boom: What's it all about?* Retrieved October 7, 2011, from http://campustechnology.com/articles/2002/11/the-electronic-portfolio-boom-whats-it-all-about.aspx

Oldest college grad. Live life: Pass it on. (n.d.). *Values.com*. Retrieved July 29, 2011, from http://www.values.com/inspirational-sayings-billboards/28-Live-Life

Straub, C. (1997). *Creating your skills portfolio: Show your skills and accomplishment*. Menlo Park, CA: Crisp Publications.

Whitaker, U. (1989). *Assessing learning: Standards, principles, and procedures*. Chicago, IL: CAEL.

## Appendices and Glossary

AACRAO. (2011). *Statement of professional ethics and practice*. Retrieved July 31, 2011, from http://www.aacrao.org/About-AACRAO/ethics-and-practice.aspx

ACE. (2011). *About ACE*. Retrieved July 31, 2011, from http://www.acenet.edu/AM/Template.cfm?Section=About_ACE

Clark, D. (2010). *Knowledge*. Used with permission. Retrieved July 31, 2011, from http://nwlink.com/~donclark/knowledge/knowledge.html

Employment and Training Administration. (2007, March). *Adult learners in higher education: Barriers to success and strategies to improve results*. Occasional paper 2007-03. Washington, DC: Author.

Lamdin, L. (1992). Earn college credit for what you know. Chicago, IL: CAEL.

# Index

## A

Accelerated courses, 27
Accomplishment, verification of, 145
Accreditation, 37, 176–77
    transfer agreements, 59
Accreditation mills, 60
ACE. *See* American Council on Education
Action plan, 30
Administrative standards, CAEL, 48
Adult-friendly colleges, 27
Adult learners
    profile, 18–22, 32, 39–40, 66, 131
    roadblocks to, 27–29
    uniqueness of, 89
Air Force transcripts, 178
American Council on Education, 3,
        61–63
    credit recommendations, 62–63
Anxiety, test-taking, 80
Appealing transcript decision, 61
Army transcripts, 178
Arts assessment, 10
Assistance in preparation, 103
Association for Legal Professionals, 63
Audience evaluation, learning
        autobiography, 118–19
Auditory learners, 79
Authenticity, 148–49
    statement of, 151–52
Autobiography
    audience evaluation, 118–19
    learning, 114–15
    organizing, 115–16

## B

Bloom's taxonomy, 97–99
Body-kinesthetic intelligence, 92

Body of narratives, 126
Bureau of Labor Statistics, 5
Business assessment, 10

## C

CAEL, 7–8
    learning assessment standards, 47–53
    National Survey on Prior Learning
        Assessment, 6
    prior learning assessment, 7–8
Candidates, 12–13
Captions, writing, 154–55
Career development, 14
    portfolio for, 160–61
    prior learning assessment, 14
Case studies, 73
Certification, 63–64, 145
    American Council on Education
        review, 63–64
    evaluation of, 65
Certifications evaluation, 8
Certified Computer Programmer, 63
Certified Novell Administrator, 63
Certified Professional Secretary, 63
Certified Purchasing Manager, 63
Challenge exams, types of, 72–73
Chartered Financial Consultant, 63
CHEA. *See* Council for Higher Education
        Accreditation
CLEP. *See* College Level Examination
        Program
Coast Guard transcripts, 179
College Board's 2010 reports, 6
College costs, 5–6
College course transcripts, request copies,
        57–58
College credit, transfer, 59–60

College Level Examination Program, 3–4, 70
College selection, 25
  criteria, 26
College-specific challenge exams, 70
  national, comparison, 74–75
Communication, effective, 34
Communications assessment, 10
Competency, testimony regarding, 145
Competency statements, 118, 140–41
Comprehensive exams, 72
Computer science assessment, 10
Concepts, knowledge of, 138–40
Conclusion to narratives, 126
Confidentiality, portfolio contents, 156
Contact information, 64
Contents of portfolio, 110–11
Copies of transcripts, 58
Core requirements, 38, 42–44
  sample worksheet, 43
Cost of college, 5–6
Council for Higher Education
  Accreditation, 59
Course descriptions, 124
  locating, 125
Course offerings, 37
Course options, verification, 34
Course research, 121–22, 182–83
Course selection, 107–8
Course syllabus, 123
Coursework planning, 33–45
  academic advisors, meeting with, 34
  accreditation, 37
  adult learner profiles, 39–40
  communication, effective, 34
  core requirements, 38, 42–44
  course offerings, 37
  course options, verification, 34
  degree-planning information,
    compiling, 34
  degree requirements, 38–40
  educational planning, 36–37
  elective credits, 41
  electives, 38, 41
  general requirements, 38, 42–44
  graduate school, 37, 45
  learning style, 37
  major requirements, 44
  majors, 38

  mapping credits, 39–40
  mapping out educational plan, 34–37
  minor requirements, 44
  minors, 38
  prior learning assessment, options, 37
  quality of education, 36
  sample worksheet, 43
  transfer credits, verification, 34
  undergraduate degree program, 38
Coursework prior learning assessment, 16
Cover sheet, 184–91
Credit by examination, 8, 68–83
  auditory learners, 79
  case studies, 73
  challenge exams, types of, 72–73
  College Level Exam Program, 70
  college-specific course challenges, 70
  demonstrations, 72
  entrance exams, 69
  experiential learning, 70
  final exams, 72
  interviews, 73
  kinesthetic learners, 79–80
  learning preferences, 78–80
  national standardized exams, 73
  placement exams, 70
  reviewing for exams, 77
  simulations, 73
  standardized national exams, 70–71
  tactile learners, 79–80
  Test of English as a Foreign Language,
    69
  test-taking anxiety, 80
  test-taking strategies, 77–78
  testing center, information available
    from, 76
  types of exams, 69–71
  visual learners, 78–79
Credits, 11–12
Critical incidents, 95–97
  description, 136
  reflection on, 97
Critical thinking, 14–15
  levels, 99
  prior learning assessment, 14–15
Cumulative grade point averages, 7
  prior learning assessment, 7
Cycle of learning, 93–95

# D

DANTES Subject Standardized Tests, 4
Definition, lead-in to, 139
Degree, time to earn, 26–27
Degree-planning information, compiling, 34
Degree requirements, 38–40
Demonstrations, 8, 72
Denial of credit, 105
Description of course, 122
Diploma mills, 15, 60
Direct sources, 145
Disagreement with assessment, 105
Distance learning, 25–26
Documentation, supporting, 8, 145–46, 148–49, 155
    gathering, 146–47
DSST. *See* DANTES Subject Standardized Tests

# E

E-mail, verification request, 150–51
E-portfolio, 157–59
    advantages, 157–58
    challenges, 158–59
Editing, 127–30
Education assessment, 10
Educational goals, 23–32
    action plan, 30
    adult-friendly colleges, 27
    adult learner, profile, 32
    case study, 31
    clarification, 24
    college selection, 25
    college selection criteria, 26
    degree, time to earn, 26–27
    distance learning, 25–26
    excerpt, 32
    flexible courses, 27
    goal, 30
    motivation, 30
    questions, 30
    roadblocks to adult learners, 27–29
    time frame, 30
    time-management activities, 28
Educational plan, 36–37
    mapping out, 34–37
Elective credits, 41

Electives, 38
    mapping, 41
Emotional IQ, 93
English assessment, 10
Entrance exams, 69
Evaluator
    guidelines, 104
    interview with, 122
Evening courses, 27
Exams, 63
    credit by, 68–83
    final, 72
    types, 69–71
Existential intelligence, 93
Experiential learning, 70, 87–89, 125–26
    challenges, 89–90
    strengths, 89–90

# F

FAA Pilot, Engineer, Mechanic Licenses, 63
Faculty evaluation, sample, 197–98
Fees for assessment, 12
Final exams, 72
Financial limitations, 15
    prior learning assessment, 15
Flexible courses, 27
Format, clarification from college on, 121
Free self-paced study resource, 80
Full credit, 105

# G

General requirements, 38
G.I. Bill, educational benefits, 179
Goals, educational, 23–32
GoArmyEd, 179
Graduate school, 37, 45
Graduation rates, 7
    prior learning assessment, 7

# H

Hybrid courses, 27

# I

Independent studies, 27
Indirect sources, 145–46

Institutions offering, 13
    prior learning assessment, 167–68
Intelligences, 92–93
    multiple, 93
International accreditation, 176–77
International transcripts, 60–61
Interpersonal intelligence, 92
Interviews, 8, 73
    with evaluator, 122
    information from, 140
    request, 105
Intrapersonal intelligence, 92
Introduction to narratives, writing, 116

## J

Job development, 14

## K

Khan Academy, 80
Kinesthetic learners, 79–80
Knowledge of concepts, in writing,
    138–40
Kolb, David, 93–95
Kolb's cycle of learning, 93–95

## L

Lead-in to definition, 139
Learning assessment standards, CAEL,
    47–53
Learning autobiography, 114–15
    audience evaluation, 118–19
    portfolio planning, audience
        evaluation, 118–19
    transitional phrases, 117
Learning chart, 113–14
Learning chronology, 111
    warm-up activities, 112–13
Learning levels, 11
Learning preferences, study strategies,
    78–80
Learning principles, study of, 87
Learning products, 145
Learning styles, 37
    test-taking strategies, 78–80
Learning theory, 87–102
    adult learners, uniqueness of, 89
    Bloom's taxonomy, 97–99
    body-kinesthetic intelligence, 92

critical incidents, 95–97
existential intelligence, 93
experiential learning, 87–90
intelligences, 92–93
interpersonal intelligence, 92
intrapersonal intelligence, 92
Kolb, David, 93–95
Kolb's cycle of learning, 93–95
learning principles, study of, 87
linguistic intelligence, 92
logical-mathematical intelligence, 92
multiple intelligences, 92–93
musical intelligence, 92
naturalistic intelligence, 92
reflection-in-action, 96–97
spatial intelligence, 92
spiritual intelligence, 93
tacit knowledge, 90–92
Learning Tree International, 63
LearningCounts.org, 7–8
Letter of verification, 149–50
    requesting, 149–51
    sample, 196
Level of learning, describing, 142–43
Levels of critical thinking, 99
Limited number of credits, prior learning
    assessment, 15
Linguistic intelligence, 92
Logical-mathematical intelligence, 92
Lower-division coursework, *vs.* upper-
    division coursework, 123–24
Lucent Technologies, Inc., 63

## M

Majors, 38
    requirements, 44
Mapping credits, 39–40
Mapping educational plan, 34–37
Marine Corps transcripts, 179
McDonald's Corporation, 63
Meeting with academic advisors, 34
Methods of assessment, 8–9
Microsoft Corporation, 63
Microsoft Office Specialist, 63
Military resources, 179
Military service, transcripts, 61–62
Military transcripts, 178–79
Military.com, 179
Mind maps, 127

Minors, 38
  requirements, 44
Montessori Associates, 63
Mortgage Bankers Association of
     America, 63
Motivation, 30
Multiple intelligences, 92–93
Musical intelligence, 92

# N

Narrative
  body of, 126
  excerpt, 184–91
  format, 126
  main points of, 127
  organization, 126, 128–29
  reference page, 140
National, college-specific exams,
     comparison, 74–75
National Guard, Yellow Ribbon Program,
     179
National standardized exams, vs. college-
     specific challenge exams, 73
Naturalistic intelligence, 92
Navy transcripts, 179
New Horizons Computer Learning
     Centers, Inc., 63

# O

Official copies, transcripts, 58
Online courses, 27
Oral presentations, 73
Organization, 121–32
Other portfolios, prior learning portfolio,
     compared, 10–11

# P

PADI International, Inc., 63
Partial credit, 105
Placement exams, 8, 70
Plagiarism, 131
Portfolio, 9–10
  table of contents, 180–81
Portfolio development, 85–164
Portfolio planning, 103–20
  assessment, disagreement with, 105
  assistance in preparation, 103

autobiography, learning, 114–16
category of learning, 108
competency statements, 118
contents, 110–11
course selection, 107–8
denial of credit, 105
evaluation, 104
evaluator guidelines, 104
full credit, 105
interview request, 105
learning autobiography, audience
     evaluation, 118–19
learning chart, 113–14
learning chronology, 111–13
partial credit, 105
preparation, 105–6
prior learning narrative, vs. college
     research paper, 117–18
refund, 104–5
significant family events, credit for,
     109
submission, 105–6
transitional phrases, learning
     autobiography, 117
travel experiences, credit for, 109
Post-training application of learning, 64
Pre-training experience, 64
Prewriting, 127, 182–83
Prior learning assessment, 1–54
  academic advisors, meeting with, 34
  accreditation, 37
  adult learner profiles, 39–40
  CAEL, 6–8
  candidates, 12–13
  career development, 14
  communication, effective, 34
  contents of portfolio, 110–11
  core requirements, 38, 42–44
  course offerings, 37
  course options, verification, 34
  coursework, 16
  credits, 11–12
  critical thinking, 14–15
  cumulative grade point averages, 7
  degree-planning information,
     compiling, 34
  degree requirements, 38–40
  educational plan, mapping out, 34–37
  educational planning, 36–37

elective credits, 41
electives, 38, 41
fees for assessment, 12
financial limitations, 15
general requirements, 38, 42–44
graduate school, 45
graduate studies, 37
graduation rates, 7
learning levels, 11
learning style, 37
limited offerings, 15
major, 38
major requirements, 44
mapping credits, 39–40
methods of assessment, 8–9
minor, 38
minor requirements, 44
money savings, 14
need for plan, 33
options, 37
portfolio of prior learning, 9–10
prior learning portfolio, *vs.* other
    portfolios, 10–11
quality of education, 36
student receives limited number of
    credits, 15
subjects assessed, 10
time savings, 7, 14
transfer credits, verification, 34
transfer limitations, 15
undergraduate degree program, 38
undergraduate degrees, 16
validation, 13–14
Prior learning inventory, 169–75
Prior learning narrative, *vs.* college
    research paper, 117–18
Prior learning portfolio, *vs.* other
    portfolios, 10–11
Problem-solving abilities, 141–42
Profile of adult learner, 18–22, 131
Program National Inst. For Automotive
    Service Excellence, 63
Proprietary information, 156–57
    protecting proprietary information,
    156–57

**Q**

Quality of education, 36

**R**

Reference page of narrative, 140
Referencing, 153–54
Reflection-in-action, 96–98
Reflection skills, 14–15
Refund, 104–5
Research, 121–32
Respiratory Therapy Technician, 63
Reviewing for exam, 77
Roadblocks to adult learners, 27–29

**S**

Savings, prior learning assessment, 14
Selecting credits to petition, 108
Selection of college, 25
Servicemembers Opportunity Colleges,
    179
Signature verification, 64
Significant family events, credit for, 109
Simulations, 8, 73
Social sciences assessment, 10
Spatial intelligence, 92
Speeches, 8
Spiritual intelligence, 93
Standard narrative format, 126
Standardized national exams, 70–71
Statement of authenticity, 151–52
Steps in learning, 136–38
Strategies for test taking, 77–78
Student receives limited number of
    credits, 15
Study strategies, learning preferences,
    78–80
Subject-matter-related materials, 122
Subjects assessed, 10
Submission, 105–6
Submitting portfolio, 160
Supporting documentation, 8, 145–46,
    148–49, 155
    authenticity, 148–49
    certifications, 145
    competence, testimony regarding, 145
    compiling, 152–53
    descriptions, 145
    direct sources, 145
    gathering, 146–47
    indirect sources, 145–46
    learning products, 145

letters of verification, 149–51
locating, 155–56
organizing, 153–54
purpose, 146
referencing, 153–54
relevance, 148
statement of authenticity, 151–52
test scores, videos of performance, 145
verification of accomplishment, 145
Syllabus course, 122
Syllabus research, 123

## T

Table of contents, portfolio of prior learning, 180–81
Tacit knowledge, 90–92
drawing from, 91
Tactile learners, 79–80
Test of English as a Foreign Language, 69
Test scores, 145
Test-taking anxiety, 80
Test-taking strategies, learning style preference, 78–80
Testimony regarding competence, 145
Testing, 55–84
Testing center, information available from, 76
Textbooks, 122
Theoretical, practical experience, linking, 91
Thought organization, 121
Three-part competency statement, 192–95
Time frame, 30
Time-management activities, 28
Time savings, 7, 14
Title of training, 64
TOEFL. *See* Test of English as a Foreign Language
Training evaluation, 8, 57–67
request sample, 64
Training providers, evaluation, 63
Transcript copies, 58
Transcripts, 55–84, 178–79
evaluation of, 57–67
official copies, 58

unofficial, 58
unofficial copies, 58
Transfer credits, 60
evaluation, 8
verification, 34
Transfer limitations, 15
Transitional phrases
examples of, 117
learning autobiography, 117
Travel experiences, credit for, 109
*Trends in College Pricing and Trends in Student Aid,* 6
Types of exams, 69–71
Types of training, American Council on Education-recommended, 62

## U

Undergraduate degrees, 16, 38
Uniqueness, adult learners, 89
Upper-division coursework, *vs.* lower-division coursework, 123–24
U.S. Bureau of Labor Statistics, 5
U.S. Postal Service, 63

## V

Verification
of accomplishment, 145
letters of, 149
sample letter of, 196
Verification clause, 64
Verification letter, 149–50
Verizon Communications, 63
Videos of performance, 145
Visual learners, 78–79

## W

Walt Disney Co., 63
Weekend classes, 27
Work sample evaluation, 8
Writing, knowledge of concepts, 138–40
Writing about learning, 133–44
Writing captions, 154–55
Writing strategies, 121–32

## Y

Yellow Ribbon Program, 179